Throughout its forty years of *apartheid*, South Africans' hope for justice required the witness of many a Jeremiah. Peter Storey was one of them. To read these pages is to learn anew what makes preaching powerful: the life and *locatedness* of the preacher. Storey has been a minister who went where the human suffering was—because that is where the God of Jesus is always going."

Donald W. Shriver, Jr. President Emeritus,
Union Theological Seminary, New York

"These sermons preached by a courageous pastor, ecumenical leader, and bishop helped transform a culturally captive congregation and a racially divided nation into a sign of God's reign of justice and compassion. *With God in the Crucible* is a means of grace and transformation to pastors, church leaders, and congregations who aspire to be faithful to the Gospel in a divided and violent world. This book is a 'must read.' "

Kenneth L. Carder, Resident Bishop Mississippi Area,
The United Methodist Church

"These extraordinary sermons, preached in the crucible of yet another of humanity's shameful periods, reveal the insight of a prophet and the care of a pastor. Peter Storey powerfully exemplifies the injunction to preach with the Bible in one hand and the daily newspaper in the other. It is rare to discover someone who has talked the talk and walked the walk with such eloquence, grace, truthfulness, and courage. *With God in the Crucible* is a powerful witness to the Gospel and a gift of hope for us all."

L. Gregory Jones, Dean of the Divinity School
and Professor of Theology, Duke University

More than sermons, *With God in the Crucible* is the journal of a prophetic soul. Peter Storey is one of the heroes of the church's struggle against *apartheid*, but this vivid memoir is not restricted to South Africa. It belongs to all of us. We have been waiting for this book a long time. Every reader will be moved and inspired by it."

Richard Lischer, author of *Open Secrets:*
A Memoir of Faith and Discovery

"Like the words of the biblical prophets, Peter's words sometimes disturb, often inspire, and always point toward the fulfillment of God's Kingdom, coming on earth, even as it is already fulfilled in heaven."

James A. Harnish, Senior Pastor,
Hyde Park United Methodist Church, Tampa, Florida

With God in the Crucible

Preaching Costly Discipleship

PETER STOREY

Abingdon Press
Nashville

WITH GOD IN THE CRUCIBLE
PREACHING COSTLY DISCIPLESHIP

This book is printed on acid-free paper.

Library of Congress Cataloging-in-Publication Data

Storey, Peter John, 1938–
    With God in the crucible : preaching costly discipleship / Peter Storey.
      p. cm.
    ISBN 0-687-05253-X (pbk.: alk. paper)
    1. Methodist Church of Southern Africa—Sermons. 2. Sermons, English—20th century. 3. Sermons, English—South Africa. I. Title.
    BX8333.S76 W58 2002
    252'.07—dc 21

                                                                      2002004402

All Scripture quotations unless otherwise noted are from *The New English Bible.* © The Delegates of the Oxford University Press and The Syndics of the Cambridge University Press 1961, 1970. Reprinted by permission.

Scripture quotations marked RSV are taken from the *Revised Standard Version of the Bible,* copyright 1946, 1952, 1971 by the Division of Christian Education of the National Council of the Churches of Christ in the United States of America. Used by permission. All rights reserved.

"Celebrate with Me" reprinted with permission from the *Book of Proceedings, 15th World Methodist Conference, 1986, Nairobi, Kenya.* World Methodist Council.

Samuel Rayan, "I beg to differ" from *Your Will be Done* (Singapore: CCA, 1984).

Extensive effort has been made to identify the owner(s) and/or administrator(s) of each copyright. The Publisher regrets any omission and will, upon written notice, make the necessary correction(s) in subsequent printings.

02 03 04 05 06 07 08 09 10 11—10 9 8 7 6 5 4 3 2 1

MANUFACTURED IN THE UNITED STATES OF AMERICA

For Elizabeth,

whose life has spoken Gospel

more clearly than all these words

Contents

Foreword

I have always been impressed with Peter Storey's way with words. He is a consummate craftsman, and this collection of sermons provides ample evidence of this. And yet it is not so much the beauty of his eloquence that I want to extol.

I have sometimes wondered whether those who live in threatening situations, confronting injustice and oppression, marginalized and made voiceless by poverty, and almost invariably without much clout—whether only such people are really able to hear the paradoxically exhilarating message of the Gospel, and that their peculiar circumstances expose them, make them particularly open, to the splendidly liberating words of the Scriptures. Their life setting is an important, indeed crucial, key to their exegesis, to their hermeneutics.

It may be that it is not just entry into the Kingdom that is problematic for the rich person. It could well be that riches, comfort, and so forth are a serious obstacle to hearing the word of God. Be that as it may, for us the Scriptures came wonderfully alive, utterly subversive of injustice and oppression. We experienced our God as Emmanuel, God with us, not giving good advice from some inaccessible Olympian fastness, but being there with us in the fiery furnace. The God who was not deaf but heard our cries of anguish because of our bondage, the God who had seen and known our suffering and who, as of old, would come down to deliver us. From the midst of this furnace Peter expounded these Scriptures, and the hearts of God's abused children thrilled to hear of the exploits of this God who was forever biased in their favor against the powerful of the land.

It was preaching such as we have examples of in this modest collection that helped to bolster the morale of God's little people and kept the light of hope flickering amidst the encircling gloom of *apartheid's* ghastly darkness. Peter Storey did this elegantly and oh, so eloquently, for it was indeed a matter of life and death in those days. That sounds almost melodramatic against the backdrop of today's stability and peace in a free and democratic South Africa. But in the bad old days it was the stark, unalloyed truth.

The second attribute I would lift up is Peter Storey's courage. He had demonstrated it when he decided that the Central Methodist Church should become nonracial. That required courage of the highest order, and he lost some two hundred white congregants. This did not deter him. It did not make him dilute the Gospel message as he understood it. To be faithful to the Gospel and its imperatives was literally a matter of life and death.

Peter Storey as president of the South African Council of Churches and I as its general secretary once went to Venda, one of the homelands, because a leading cleric had been detained without trial there. We got an icy welcome from the security establishment who bristled with anger and hostility, and we were unceremoniously bundled off into the bush and then to a nonexistent border with South Africa and deported! When we were safely in our car and had got away, we both heaved huge sighs of relief. I said, "You know they could have killed us."

We did not know then just how close we had been to our deaths. After the Truth and Reconciliation process, a former white military officer who had been seconded to the Venda homeland security establishment told Storey and me that he needed to ask our forgiveness. He told us that he had given orders for us to be killed on that occasion and still didn't know why they had not been carried out.

It is out of this crucible that Storey's sermons were forged, and that gives them an authenticity that is gained only through running the gauntlet of the wrath of the powerful. He did and lived to tell the tale.

Desmond Tutu
Archbishop Emeritus
of Cape Town

Preface

All my life, I have been moved by preachers who were unafraid to take on the world.

My father was a loved pastor and a preacher of depth and sensitivity, whose sermons glowed with the beauty and nobility of Christ. The Jesus he preached was the Jesus I came to love. In the early 1950s he discerned that the newly elected *apartheid* government in South Africa was driven by an idolatry of race and nation not much different from that of Nazism. As a Cape Town schoolboy sitting with my friends in the back pew, I became aware of the discomfort among many in the congregation, and the unpopularity it brought him when he contrasted the way of Jesus with the increasingly hateful ways of our nation. He became the first Church leader to publicly denounce *apartheid* as a sin against God, earning the ire of its architect, Dr. H. F. Verwoerd. As leader of the Methodist Church in South Africa in 1957, he continued this strong stand; but two years later he died of heart disease. I wish he had lived longer; but his life taught me that depth of integrity, not length of years, is what counts, and that the cost of truth telling will be high, but nothing less is expected of the preacher.

Australian preacher Alan Walker led evangelistic missions in Cape Town and Pretoria in 1963 and shocked many by combining deeply personal altar calls with stinging critiques of our nation's *apartheid* practices. Here was preaching that liberated the Gospel from privatized piety without diluting its personal claim on the human will. It was the kind of proclamation I believed could make a difference. For two years I saw him at work in his own homeland, never failing to offer the call to personal discipleship, never flinching from the lonely task of proclaiming social justice. Walker believed that the mind-set of societies and cultures could and should be influenced by faithful proclamation, and seldom has there been a preacher anywhere whose words on a Sunday were so closely studied in the places of power on Monday.

Desmond Tutu's courageous tenure as general secretary of the South African Council of Churches, and my years as its president, threw us together at the sharp end of the church-state conflict when it was at its height. We worked closely under enormous stress and shared some tight corners, at least one of which we were fortunate to survive. When we differed, it was with deep respect. I honor him for his iron discipline of prayer and devotion, the spiritual center without which no prophet can be faithful, and for proving that we need look no further than Scripture and the central doctrines of the faith as the ground on which to stand for truth and justice. Theology, rather than ideology, fueled his witness, making the difference between bold prophecy in the biblical tradition and utopian political activism. It also freed him to respond to situations with grace-filled spontaneity. Desmond Tutu had a way of reminding us that God was not very impressed with those who seemed so powerful, but that this same God could be incredibly generous with undeserving people.

I was fortunate to encounter other contemporary prophets personally, including Martin Niemöller, Donald Soper, Clarence Jordan, and of course, Beyers Naude. Dietrich Bonhoeffer was required reading for those of us who connected what was happening in South Africa with the recent Hitler years.

All these prophets had this in common: They understood that they needed to take on the world because that is what the Gospel does. The idea that Jesus came simply to assure a satisfactory passage for individuals through this life is as absurd as it is self-absorbed. It does an injustice to the Incarnation and cheapens the cross. The notion that the Church is a place only for spiritual deepening, character-building, mutual care and service ignores Jesus' core message, the return of a rebel world to its rightful owner and the inauguration of a new reign of justice and peace. It was commitment to this cosmic enterprise that got Jesus crucified, and modern disciples of the Crucified One should know that, in this respect, the world has not become any more Gospel-friendly.

—m—

Some parts of the world are, of course, more unfriendly than others; and when these sermons were preached, this was certainly true of my homeland, South Africa.

South Africa had been under white rule since 1652; but in 1948, when it should have joined the world movement to end colonialism, South Africa's white minority elected a regime determined to stop the march of history. They promised perpetual white domination with something they called *apartheid*, the crudest possible form of race discrimination.

By the time I entered seminary in 1957, the ugly building blocks of *apartheid* were well in place. Race Classification had defined all of us according to our color. Whites like me carried neat plastic cards, people of Asian or mixed-race ("colored") background were also painstakingly classified, and blacks carried a many-paged "Pass Book" to control their movements each day. Residential separation was legislated, every city and town in South Africa dissected into White, "Colored," Asian, and Bantu (Black African) "Group Areas," and the process of evicting people had begun. Later, under the much more ambitious "Bantu Homelands" policy, inhospitable rural areas were declared to be tribal homelands, and three and a half million black people were removed from the cities or their historic rural homes and dumped in these places.

The future subjugation of people of color was built into their own education. Laws regarding "Job Reservation" preserved most high paying work for whites. Another pillar of the *apartheid* edifice was social segregation similar to that practiced in the American South. Mixed restaurants, cinemas, post office counters, elevators, park benches, et al., were forbidden. Sex across the color line, whether casual or within the sacred bonds of marriage, was the ultimate taboo, enforced by the "Immorality Act," that turned police officers into invasive bedroom voyeurs.

All these indignities could not be implemented without massive repression, so the machinery of a police state steadily grew. Beneath the trappings of a limited Western democracy, there emerged a degree of secret police control that would have made the Soviets proud. When resistance began to burgeon in 1960, black political leadership was exiled or imprisoned, and whites were conscripted and militarized. White school children were indoctrinated with "Christian National Education," convincing them of their manifest destiny as the guardians of Christian (for that, read *white*) values in Africa, against both Eastern-bloc Communism and Western liberalism.

Apartheid and the structures that buttressed it would become all-pervasive. Our faithfulness to Christ, whether we liked it or not, would be defined by our response to this massive evil. In 1957, long before all the regime's plans were in place, my father had laid out the options:

> The view of the government is that while one black person and one white person are friends, it will have failed. The view of the church is that while one black person and one white person are enemies, we will have failed. The choice is clear, God or Caesar, and we will not place the church at the disposal of the state.[1]

That same year, with other seminarians, I participated in my first act of protest—a march against university segregation. I could not have dreamed that my last such march would be a full thirty-two years later.

This collection concerns the time between, especially the years 1976 to 1994 when the struggle for South Africa's freedom was most intense.

After ordination, and two years studying city ministry with Alan Walker in Sydney, Australia, I was appointed to the Inner City Methodist Mission, in Cape Town's "Colored" or mixed-race community of District Six. Most sermon records from that precious five years have been lost, but not the lessons learned there. Through the people of District Six, God helped me to touch the painful edges of what it meant *not to be white* in South Africa, and they also permitted me to join them in their struggle for dignity. Only the closing sermon in this book is directly linked with those days; but it bridges the entire collection, linking a long ago, seemingly hopeless act of defiance with the coming of freedom.

Another period with no written sermons was a two-year stint as part-time chaplain to Robben Island prison, which enabled me to minister to political prisoners like Nelson Mandela and others of

the African National Congress, in the earliest years of their con-
finement, as well as Pan Africanist Congress leader Robert
Sobukwe. I purposely never carried written material, and my
extemporaneous sermons were responses to the circumstances I
found on the island. Usually I was only permitted to walk up and
down the long corridor and look into the cells as I preached; but on
the one occasion I was able to arrange for Mandela and the others
to be released into a sunny exercise yard for a service, the text that
seemed most appropriate was, "If the Son sets you free, you are
free indeed." The prisoners saw the pun, even if their guards did
not. In any case, my security clearance to minister on the island
was revoked by the Minister of Law and Order.

Most of the sermons in this collection were preached in the
Central Methodist Mission (CMM), the large downtown church in
the heart of Johannesburg, where I was senior pastor from 1976 to
1989. During those years, there were also wider responsibilities
and other platforms from which to preach: president of the South
African Council of Churches, president (or presiding bishop) of the
Methodist Church of Southern Africa, bishop of the Johannesburg-
Soweto area, as well as frequent international involvements. In
1990 I regretfully left CMM to concentrate fully on my responsibilities as bishop, and some sermons are from that latter period.

Ultimately, however, the preaching that counts most is not from
the platforms of great conferences, but in the journey a pastor
makes with his or her people. Those who were most fully part of
this preaching were the CMM church family. Sermons live only
when both preacher and hearers partner God in bringing them to
birth; and that wonderful, multicolored community of loyal and
courageous disciples were remarkable midwives of the Gospel. So
many of them were engaged in costly service and struggle to transform South Africa, and they came to worship hungry for the good
news, often unaware of how much their lives and witness nour-
ished the preacher. They faced security police invasions of services,
bomb-scares, and other forms of intimidation, yet their joy in
Christ overflowed. They determined to be a sign of God's future
for all our land.

It is difficult to recapture the extremes of tension, fear, and hostility experienced by those involved in resistance to the *apartheid*
regime at the time. The Truth and Reconciliation Commission has

chronicled the terror unleashed on some of the regime's opponents; and compared to that, most of us Church leaders got off lightly. The government's fear of world opinion limited action against us to phone-tapping, paying clergy colleagues to inform on us, death threats, smear campaigns, and the occasional arrest. A few were detained without trial and others banned.

Nevertheless, I have since found that there are no unwounded veterans of that struggle. In addition to the ongoing pressure of state intimidation, constant close encounters with violence-laden situations on the streets of the war-torn townships took their toll; and each day brought new crises demanding faithful response. Sadly, the struggle had to be waged on two fronts because many members and some clergy in our own churches would have preferred us to be silent. I found nothing so draining as the abusive calls and letters from people who claimed to be members of my denomination. It has been easier to understand the state security soldier who once ordered my death than to accept that faithful Methodist people could have supported *apartheid*.

The witness of the Church in South Africa's struggle has been recognized as a remarkable one. The world has honored that witness with a Nobel Peace Prize to Desmond Tutu, and Nelson Mandela has been profuse in his thanks to the churches for their leadership of the struggle while leaders like him were in prison or exile.

Yet, if we are honest, it was a minority witness, even within the denominations that officially opposed *apartheid*. Most clergy, black and white, some fearing the authorities, others fearing their congregations, were silent. Every Sunday, their sermons said everything, and nothing; they could have been preaching anywhere in the world, or nowhere in the world. They told the old, old story of Jesus and his love as if it had happened on another planet. Instead of exposing the agony of the cross planted in the soil of South Africa, worship was a shield from reality, and therefore from both the judgement and grace of God's word.

Why? How could this be? Where did we lose the passionate belief that the Gospel is given so that God's justice and peace might reign on earth as in heaven? How did we manage to so domesticate Jesus—and Moses and Isaiah, Esther and Ruth, Jeremiah and Amos, Elizabeth and Mary, Paul, Peter, John and James—that their radical demands for counterliving could melt so meekly into our cultural scene and accommodate with such servility to the demands of our Caesars?

If our task as preachers is limited to nurturing a community fixated on their own spiritual health, while occasionally offering deeds of kindness in an unkind world, then the world should thank us for entombing Jesus in our church parlors and Sunday schools and sanctuaries. That way it can go on doing whatever it wants, unencumbered by conscience, and undisturbed by the Risen Christ.

Surely that is not the way it should be! Surely we *must* take on the world!

The miracle South African Christians have to proclaim is not the story of their faithfulness; it is the wonder of a God who could use such a feeble witness so powerfully. And the question must arise, "What if the witness had been stronger? What could God not do with a truly faithful Church, willing to take on the world?"

This is not to speak of cheap triumphalism. The long years of witness in South Africa were without any guarantees, and hope often seemed dead. When our prophets spoke, those in power did not tremble—they discussed how to silence them. That it was given to us to see a new day of liberation is a great gift—the joy of it is hard to describe; but new dispensations do not change the obligation to speak truth to power. Caesar may have a kinder, gentler face, but Caesar is still Caesar.

If the words in this collection are to have any contemporary relevance, this is where I hope it may be found. No nation, no culture, can escape the furnace of testing. The forces that almost destroyed South Africa are dangerously alive in every society, biding their time and waiting to be unleashed. The search for what the Bible calls righteousness, or "compassionate fair-dealing," will remain unfinished so long as Christians anywhere pray for God's will to be done on earth as in heaven, and take those words seriously.

In *apartheid* South Africa we were inspired to hope by the words and actions of other Christians, facing the searing heat of other cauldrons. Our small ounces of courage came from knowing that, in other places of pain and oppression, there were those who were unafraid to confront their Caesars with God's demand for justice. The witness of faithful and prophetic Christians—in East Germany; or on the roads of Georgia, Mississippi, and Alabama; in the streets of Manila; or in the villages of Guatemala and El Salvador—braced our fainting spirits.

Frail though our witness was, now that our ordeal is over, we owe it to others to tell them, "When your time of testing comes, please remember that we have a great God! Please trust this great God more faithfully and fearlessly than we did."

In the book of Daniel those wonderful three stalwarts, Shadrach, Meshach, and Abed-nego were ultimately rescued from the burning, fiery furnace; but that is not the point of the story. The book of Hebrews tells us of hundreds who were *not* delivered from their encounters with the powers of this world. The point of the Daniel story lies in those quiet words spoken to the ruler who wanted their worship:

> *If there is a god who is able to save us from the blazing furnace, it is our God whom we serve, and he will save us from your power, O king;* but if not, *be it known to your majesty that we will neither serve your god nor worship the golden image that you have set up.* (Daniel: 3:17-18, emphasis added)

That is the witness required of us. Whether in places of brutal oppression, as *apartheid* South Africa was, or places where more respectable and apparently religious Caesars seek to coopt the Church rather than oppress it, that is all that is required of us. We can trust God with the rest.

---

1. Clifford K. Storey, Presidential Address, Methodist Conference, East London, October 1957.

Acknowledgments

My thanks to those who cajoled me to assemble this collection. Will Willimon suggested it first in 1987, and Greg Jones, my dean, has made it his theme since I joined Duke Divinity School in 1999. Thanks to each of them, and to Rick Lischer and James Harnish for reading drafts and offering helpful advice. Ned Dewire and Jim Waits also nudged me patiently over the years and they, together with Elizabeth and our four sons, who have been very patient, will be glad that it is done. My editor at Abingdon Press has been an encouragement and delight to work with.

What Desmond Tutu and Will Willimon have written here is undeserved. I humbly thank them.

My special thanks to those congregations among whom I ministered, and for the high privilege of being permitted to mount the pulpit week by week to break the bread of life with them.

1

Which Way South Africa?

Address from the Public Issues Platform,
Central Methodist Mission, Sydney, Australia,
November 1966

In 1965 our small family left South Africa's shores for the first time, for Sydney, Australia. I joined the staff of the Central Methodist Mission there to study city ministry for two years under the tutelage of Dr. Alan Walker,[1] one of the great preachers and urban pastors of the twentieth century. While we were there, *apartheid*'s chief ideologue, Prime Minister H. F. Verwoerd, was assassinated in the Cape Town Parliament. He was succeeded by the iron-fisted John Vorster, who compounded the insults of *apartheid* with the first "detention without trial" legislation, taking South Africa further down the road to police state rule.

As we prepared to return home, two convictions were becoming clear: The first was that God was calling us to ministry in the inner city. The second was that no ministry in South Africa could have integrity unless it confronted *apartheid* head-on in the name of Christ. These two convictions would shape our future.

Shortly before we left for home, Alan Walker invited me to use his public issues platform to address the South African situation. I include this address because it contains seeds of those convictions that would develop and hold me accountable throughout the struggle years.

—𝕞—

W hen I speak of South Africa, I speak of a land that to know is to love. When I speak of South African people, I can see faces, black and white faces, family and friends; and I speak of myself too. When I speak of the sin and agony of South Africa, I speak of something in which I share.

There come moments in the history of a nation when the whole future direction of its affairs can depend on a few climactic events. The issues seem to divide, and there are two roads. One road beckons forward and upward to a new destiny under God, and the other leads backwards and downwards to a frightening nowhere. God has told us of such moments, but God doesn't write them in the sky. It is for people of sensitivity and prophetic insight to recognize them when they come and to discern the alternatives and their consequences.

Clearly, for South Africa such a moment came when a choice had to be made to stride out courageously into a great experiment of nonracial democracy or to retreat into a black night of fear and suppression. Equally clear is the fact that that moment has passed. Some recognized it and cried out, but they were not in the seats of power and their words fell on ears deafened by the catch phrases of self-interest and prejudice. In South Africa the choice was made when in a new postwar world a government was elected that pledged itself to eternal division and domination. For nearly two decades now, we have seen them proceed with blind determination and ruthlessness such as only those driven by self-interest can be capable of.

The recent assassination of Prime Minister H. F. Verwoerd[2] is something that only fools will welcome: a meaningless, useless, depraved act—as are all acts of violence. It is certain to unleash more bitterness into a community already sick to its soul. When we remember that the leaders of Afrikaner nationalism have never been merely politicians, but are viewed as the high priests of a racist ideology, the consequences of such an act are likely to be emotional as well as political, making clear and honest thinking even more difficult.

Dr. Verwoerd's successor has no benevolent and fatherly image; neither has he the same measure of intellectual brilliance. It is unlikely that he will be able as cleverly to tread the razor edge of international statecraft (so important if South Africa is to remain undisturbed by an inquisitive world). Mr. Vorster is not as adept at creating smokescreens, nor has he ever tried to. He is a man of immense personal influence and emotion, and he possesses a demagogue's power to sway people. As an orator he is capable of expressing almost religiously the creed of Afrikaner nationalism.

Which Way South Africa?

The way looks stormy indeed, *but I am a Christian and Christians believe that the roots of politics are always deeper than politics.* We are not dealing merely with this or that policy when we place the South African crisis into a Christian context; we are faced with the same battle as are Christians everywhere—in Poland or East Germany or Alabama or Australia. We are grappling with unredeemed human nature and the way it behaves when its interests are threatened. The South African crisis is a crisis for Christianity and for all who name the name of Christ, anywhere.

In the political sense the moment of choice may have passed. In human terms it would appear that nothing can arrest the downward slide. But God has given a promise that if God's people anywhere hear God's voice and turn to choose the road of obedience, even if they have failed in the past, a new dimension can invade the vicious circle of our folly and fear to "heal the land." It is this promise that is the only hope for South Africa in the immediate future. This promise must become the watchword of South African Christians in the present hour.

When I speak of God's Church, I speak of people in every denomination—black and white. I speak not only of conferences and assemblies whose words have rung rather hollow of late. I speak of those in every group who will see that the claims of Christ must be held above the claims of nationalism and race. I see emerging out of Christ's crucible in South Africa a new "Confessing Church" drawn from Roman Catholics, Methodists, Anglicans—in fact every denomination including (and most significant) the Dutch Reformed Church,[3] whose united witness will be to confess the lordship of Christ over the claims of Caesar. I believe that this "new body" is already painfully taking shape in movements like the Christian Institute founded by Dutch Reformed minister Beyers Naude.[4]

The predictable comment on this would be that it has all come rather late. It is late—terribly late, and I could spend time analyzing some of the reasons for this. But the question is whether any move in the right direction is too late for God to make use of. Late as it is, perhaps it is not *too* late. I believe that Christ's Church in South Africa will answer his call to a task of costly redemption in a sick society. In the years ahead I see three great patterns of ministry for the South African Church:

- The Church must prepare to be the only consistent witness to the Gospel truths about humanity and God. The essence of free speech lies not only in the freedom to say what you like (a freedom most Christians still hold in South Africa) but also in the right to be heard publicly and widely. With radio in government hands and newspapers increasingly hemmed in with intimidating legislation, this second freedom is no longer fully enjoyed. Consequently the bravest and wisest statements never filter through to the mass of the population. In a nation where the mass media is almost totally controlled by the state, where only a few English-speaking newspapers valiantly struggle to maintain their integrity in the face of intimidation, where politicians in high places speak openly of the "excellent progress of conditioning our people," Christian Churches, schools (where we still have them), and Sunday schools attain a new significance. They must become enclaves where the brains of people can become "unwashed"; where the minds of children can be garrisoned against the prevailing forces of state-sponsored "Christian-national" education; where truth must combat the accepted myths of racism and "*baaskap*."[5]
- The Church will be the last preserve of genuine inter-racial contact on a basis other than the master-servant

relationship. It must fight to be the place where we can still grasp the hand of people of a different color to discover that they are human and possessed together of the same hopes and fears, joys and sorrows. The Church must be the community where South Africans will find that although they are of different color, their heart hungers are the same.

- The Church must fashion a program to fully identify herself through service with those who suffer daily from the economic, material, and emotional consequences of enforced *apartheid*. In a nation where there are more than eight thousand prisoners of conscience, where more than one thousand people have been detained for periods without trial, where "group area" legislation moves thousands arbitrarily from one place to another, where "influx control" separates husbands from wives and children, Christ's Church is called to engage to a far greater extent in the ministry of feeding the hungry, clothing the naked, visiting the captive and the sick. In a nation where the oppressed are becoming progressively disillusioned with a talking Christianity, Jesus the Healer must be manifested through a far greater invasion of Christian concern in among the sufferers.

The Church must acknowledge the failure and half-heartedness of her recent protests and must energetically explore new paths of Christian resistance. There can be few more damning indictments of the Church than the statement by a Communist that he joined the Communist Party "because they were the only group in South Africa who were prepared to suffer."

Christ's "Confessing Church" must accept her destiny to take the initiative out of the hands of those who think in the archaic and tragic language of violence. Bloodshed and violence on a massive scale will not be avoided by crying "Peace, peace, when there is no peace." It will only be staved off by the injection of a new force for social change into the dilemma. Some form of nonviolent Christian action must speak where words have failed.

This could only issue out of a great call to repentance, which would, I believe, be heeded by far more white people than most outsiders would think possible. There is a great yearning to be rid of the guilt of the years, and it is not impossible for God to make the yearning for righteousness greater than a person's fear.

The shape of any program of nonviolent resistance would, I suppose, be peculiarly South African; it would have to be utterly Christian in motive. I do not know what its chances would be to actually bring social change, but I remember with hope, that Mahatma Gandhi won his first great victory with "soul-force" on the roads of Natal in South Africa.

Which way South Africa? I believe that the answer will be found in the urgency of another question: *"Which way the Church of Jesus Christ in South Africa?"* My prayer is that she will see her moment of destiny and gladly embrace whatever suffering it may involve. If she does, then my certainty is that, come what may, neither Vorster, nor racism, nor nationalism, nor even the gates of hell shall prevail against her.

---

1. Now Reverend Sir Alan Walker, former superintendent of the Central Methodist Mission, Sydney, Australia. He had conducted a controversial preaching mission in South Africa in 1963, castigating *apartheid*. I had raised the possibility of learning more from him. He invited me to join the Mission staff as director of one of its ministries, the world's first Life Line Center.

2. Verwoerd, the ideologue who determined to take *apartheid* to every possible extreme, was stabbed to death in the South African Parliament by an apparently deranged Parliamentary messenger in 1966.

3. The Dutch Reformed family of Churches gave consistent theological support to the ideology of *apartheid*, but there were courageous exceptions among their clergy.

4. Reverend C. F. Beyers Naude was hounded out of the Dutch Reformed Church after he challenged its support of the ideology of *apartheid*. He went on to found the Christian Institute (CI) and to become one of the great Christian witnesses against the *apartheid* state.

5. Afrikaans word, literally "being the boss"—the policy of domination.

2

Christ's Peacemakers

South African Council of Churches Commitment Service
Central Methodist Church
Sunday before the Soweto Shootings, June 13, 1976

They have healed the wound of my people lightly, saying, "Peace, peace," when there is no peace. (Jeremiah 8:11 RSV)

How blest are the peacemakers; God shall call them his sons. (Matthew 5:9)

In January 1976, after serving for five years in District Six, Cape Town, and four years pastoring a student church in Johannesburg, I was appointed senior pastor of the Central Methodist Church in downtown Johannesburg. It was an honor, with added meaning for me because my father was converted there in the 1920s and had been the first candidate for ordination to come from its congregation. "Central," as everybody knew it, was South African Methodism's premier pulpit. The congregation had been founded in 1886, on the gold diggings on the South African *veld* that later became the new city of Johannesburg.

In its early days, it had operated like the great Central Halls of England and Australia—offering powerful evangelical preaching, while engaging the poor with ministries of social care. Over the years, however, Central Church had become an increasingly "First Church"–type congregation

27

priding itself more on the number of mayors it had produced than ministries. Like most Methodist Churches of the day, it was open in theory and segregated in practice. I came to its pulpit convinced that this great Church needed to return to its first love—the poor of the city—and that we could have little prophetic impact on the culture of *apartheid* unless our membership was racially inclusive. These convictions would lead to radical changes at Central Church, but they would take time to unfold.

The service where this sermon was preached was the first attended by a significant number of black people. Six months into this new appointment, I was asked to conduct a Service of Commitment for the staff of the South African Council of Churches (SACC), who were becoming increasingly the target of state pressure. The SACC was leading church opposition to the *apartheid* regime's deeply resented policies on black education. They needed encouragement.

None of us knew that three days after this service the political landscape of South Africa would change forever.

—⟶⟶—

In welcoming the officers and staff of the South African Council of Churches tonight I am mindful of the purpose to which the SACC, representing the majority of Christians in this land, is called. You are called to "foster the unity of Christians in South Africa, and to further the Kingdom of God by so doing."[1] That search for Christian unity goes on.

Recently, however, an even greater priority has pressed upon you: that of bearing witness to the *wider unity* God wants for *all* God's children. You have been inexorably drawn into the struggle for justice and reconciliation between the people of this land, the struggle for South Africa's soul.

Your commitment to this struggle has brought unpopularity. You have suffered public smears by the South African Broadcasting Corporation and private persecution by the security police. Please know today that your stand has also brought the everlasting gratitude of countless "little people" in this land who thank God for your caring.

There is no group of people more realistically and extensively working for peaceful change in South Africa today than the SACC. Of you, I believe Jesus would want to say, *"How blest are the peacemakers; God shall call them his sons"—and daughters* (Matthew 5:9).

Jesus, the Prince of Peace, and Son of God, calls those who work for peace his brothers and sisters. Those who stand in a divided world, pointing the way to unity; those who live in a hateful world, demonstrating the way of love; those who share with Jesus the ministry of reconciliation; these are the people most closely related to him. In these days when only the work of the peacemaker can avert terrible strife, this great task is not just for you, but for all of us who name the name of Christ.

Who, then, are Christ's peacemakers? How shall we know them? How shall we too become peacemakers with Jesus?

Called by God

Hundreds of years before Christ, in an encounter with the living God, a young man was told that before he had been formed in the womb, already he was marked to be a prophet. He protested that he was a mere child, but God spoke sternly to him:

> *Do not call yourself a child; for you shall go to whatever people I send you and say whatever I tell you to say. Fear none of them, for I am with you and will keep you safe.* (Jeremiah 1:7, 8)

It was the experience of this encounter with God that called Jeremiah to offer himself as messenger to a stubborn nation. From then on he was on a new road with new priorities. In the midst of deep suffering and struggle, he was to say that the word of the Lord was like *"a fire blazing in my heart"* (Jeremiah 20:9), something he could never put out.

In times of confusion and conflict, it is only when we are touched by the eternal that we know what to do in the here and now. My prayer for you, in this time of deep crisis, is that you will know that you also are called by God. I pray that you too will know that fire in your heart, driving you to do what God wants in our land.

Not Fooled by False Peace

The prophet Jeremiah's burden was that he was sent among deluded people. They thought all was well when nothing was well. They thought they were healthy when they were deathly sick. That is why he cries out against the religious of his day, saying, *"They have healed the wound of my people lightly"* (RSV)—the New English Bible says, *"they dress my people's wound, but skin-deep only" (8:11)*— *"saying, 'Peace, peace,' when there is no peace"* (RSV).

Among those who think all is well in South Africa, the prophet also has this thankless task. There is a deep delusion that we live in peace.

For evidence of this desperate self-delusion, think back to SABCTV's[2] presentation on Republic Day less than a week ago.[3] What they said was not necessarily untrue, but *what they didn't say* cried out mutely to be heard.

Behind this glib self-congratulation and pious glorification of one people's nationalism, I heard the cry of the wronged and the bitterness of the oppressed:

- those whose land has been taken away;
- those whose family life has been ripped apart for the security of others;
- those whose voices have been stilled by vicious laws;
- those whose brains and bodies are stunted by poor education and poverty.

What a travesty of truth! What a price to pay for our Republic! Think of the *Baralong Ba Ga Matlabe* tribe who, in return for their loyal services to the Boer Republic of Transvaal, were given freehold land by President Paul Kruger in 1885. Now you will find them living in a tattered tent-town called *Rooigrond,* hounded out by descendants of Kruger's white tribe, the Potchefstroom Town Council,[4] in 1970.

Need I remind you of the removal of Sophiatown or District Six in Cape Town?

What price our Republic? Jeremiah would call it a *"cracked cistern that can hold no water"* (Jeremiah 2:13).

"'Peace, peace,' when there is no peace."

The choice before us today is not that of *peace* or *violence*; that is too simplistic. It is between creating a *real* peace rooted in justice for all or having people rise up with violence to *escape the violence that is breaking them now.*

The precondition for making real peace is facing the truth. It is only those who have seen God's vision for us all who cannot be deceived. Such people will continue to move among the blind, the deaf, the satisfied, and cry:

> *This is the nation that did not obey the Lord its God nor accept correction; truth has perished, it is heard no more on their lips.* (Jeremiah 7:28)

If we are to be called the children of God, we must stop being deceived. True peacemakers will face the truth that South Africa's peace is a false peace.

Seeking to Be What We Believe

If we are to be Christ's peacemakers, then we must learn his ways. The uniqueness of Jesus lay not only in what he said but in who he was and how he lived. In his life the congruence between word and deed was absolute, and because of that he could be the supreme peacemaker, breaking down the "dividing wall" that divides us from God and from each other (Ephesians 2:14).

This must be the mark of Christ's peacemakers also. The giants of history are those who have put high principle not only into words but action. They lived as visible examples, signs of what they cherished for all people. In a world of cynicism, where the ugly and selfish dimensions of human nature are too often uppermost, there is something surprising and beautiful about a *living example of the difference.*

Racism is a disease of the heart; it is rooted in the fear that casts out love; it cannot be divorced from our selfishness and pride. That is why we cannot be Christ's peacemakers in this land unless our inward spirits begin to match our outward ideals. People must be able to look at how we live and say: *"Perhaps it is possible for people to repent of their divisions, to come together and work and pray and struggle together, and to live a common life."* Christ's peacemakers must be signs of hope.

It is said of the Japanese saint Toyohiko Kagawa that the sermon he preached most often was one of utter simplicity: "God is love," he used to say, standing on street corners, "God is love, like Jesus."

- For Jesus, there could be no secret plotting and maneuvering to achieve his aims;
- For Jesus, the end never justified the means;
- For Jesus, there could be no use of evil to overcome evil.

Though his agenda was to save a whole world, he would rather fail than lose his integrity. "What is the profit for a man who gains the whole world at the price of his soul?"

We must be like Jesus. We must be transparent people. We must *be what we believe.*

When he was strengthening his own peacemakers to face those who willed them harm, Martin Luther King, Jr. called for the same congruence of profession and practice, the same transparency of heart:

> Love must be your regulating ideal. Once again we must hear the words of Jesus echoing across the centuries: "Love your enemies, bless them that curse you, and pray for them that despitefully use you." If we fail to do this our protest will end up as a meaningless drama on the stage of history, and its memory will be shrouded with the ugly garments of shame. . . . If you will protest courageously, and yet with dignity and Christian love, . . . the historians will . . . say, "There lived a great people—a black people—who injected new meaning and dignity into the veins of civilization."[5]

We must *be* what we believe.

Strengthened by God's Promise

How do we find the strength to be peacemakers? What was it that nerved Jeremiah in his times of deep despair? It was the promise of the living God, a promise not only to be with Jeremiah, but to be his strength:

This day I make you a fortified city,
  a pillar of iron, a wall of bronze,
  to stand fast against the whole land,
against the kings and princes of Judah,
  its priests and its people.
  They will make war upon you but shall not overcome you,
for I am with you and will keep you safe.
  This is the very word of the LORD. (Jeremiah 1:18, 19)

It has been given to only a few of God's prophets to see the results of their witness. Moses didn't. Jeremiah didn't. Nor did some of God's modern witnesses—peacemakers like Martin Luther King, Jr. and Albert Luthuli. Yet they remained true. They did so because their strength was in God. They could give themselves wholly to the struggle for real peace, justice, and reconciliation because it was God who steeled their determination and God who would not cease to work, even when they could labor no more.

For them it was sufficient to know that they had played their part as the brothers and sisters of Jesus, children of God, peacemakers.

Strengthened by God's promise, we must do the same.

---

1. From the Constitution of the South African Council of Churches at the time.

2. South African Broadcasting Corporation's television arm. The SABC was state-controlled and used shamelessly as a tool of government propaganda.

3. Under *apartheid*, May 31 each year was celebrated by supporters of the regime as "Republic Day," commemorating the declaration of a Republic and withdrawal from the British Commonwealth of Nations in 1961.

4. All examples of *apartheid's* Forced Removals policy. Potchefstroom is a town about one hundred kilometers southwest of Johannesburg. Sophiatown was a black freehold suburb in Johannesburg. District Six was the traditional home of the mixed race, or "Colored" people of Cape Town. In all these places people were hounded out because of the color of their skin.

5. Martin Luther King, Jr., quoted by Lerone Bennett, Jr., in *What Manner of Man: A Biography of Martin Luther King, Jr., 1929–1968* (Chicago: Johnson Publishing, 1968), 65-66.

3

The Blood Has Been Shed

Central Methodist Church, Johannesburg
Sunday after the Soweto Shootings, June 20, 1976

Would that my head were all water,
my eyes a fountain of tears,
that I might weep day and night
for my people's dead! (Jeremiah 9: 1)

On Wednesday, June 16, just three days after the SACC Commitment Service, thousands of Soweto school children, fed up with having to study in the hated Afrikaans language, marched in protest. Their massive, nonviolent action, took the authorities by surprise. In their first confrontation with the police, they were met by bullets. Numbers of youths were killed, while others reacted with a rampage, burning government buildings in Soweto. In the next few months, hundreds of black youths died at the hands of the police.

The days following June 16 were a blur of crisis meetings, emergency parents' committees, telephone confrontations with Prime Minister Vorster,[1] the setting up of an international fund for victims, and more reports of police shootings. It was not a week conducive to quiet reflection.

This sermon was preached to a half empty church. Numbers of members, angered by the presence of many black persons in worship the week before as well as the sermon content, boycotted the service. They preferred to get their news of the crisis from the government controlled mass media.

The honeymoon at Central Methodist Church was over. In the years ahead the struggle to become an integrated congregation and to address the real issues in our land would cost us some two hundred of our nine hundred white members.

—᷍᷍᷍—

Since we last met, things have happened that must surely have such an impact upon us that we will never be the same. Last week, by a strange and terrible coincidence, we were thinking of the words of Jeremiah, *"They have healed the wound of my people lightly, saying 'Peace, peace,' when there is no peace"* (Jeremiah 8:11 RSV).

Now, because of what happened last Wednesday, other words of that same prophet invade our minds:

> *For the wound of the daughter of my people is my*
> *heart wounded,*
> *I mourn, and dismay has taken hold on me.*
> *Is there no balm in Gilead?*
> *Is there no physician there?* (Jeremiah 8:21-22 RSV)

> *O that my head were waters,*
> *and my eyes a fountain of tears,*
> *that I might weep day and night*
> *for the slain of the daughter of my people!*
> (Jeremiah 9:1 RSV)

Last week I said that we had a choice between creating a real peace for all, based on facing the truth—or having people rise up against the violence that is breaking them. Some of you protested that those words were too dramatic. Now we see, God help us, that they were not strong enough. In the horrors of Wednesday, just three days after they were spoken, the choice was made.

Last week, with our guests being staff persons of the South African Council of Churches, I preached about the cost of being peacemakers, because that is the task they felt deeply called to.

Some spoke to me afterward and thanked me, because they said my words had given them hope. Now I have seen many of those same people, haggard, drawn, and brokenhearted as their striving for peaceful change has been drowned out by violence. Yet still they have worked on, risking their lives to come out of Soweto to report what is happening and confront the authorities, risking their lives again to go back and stand between their people and the police, pleading for an end to the violence of both.

And now, added to the cries for justice that the government refused to hear, is the wailing of the bereaved and the silence of the dead. The message is now written in blood. God forgive us if we do not hear it now.

What does this blood say to us?

Care While Caring Is Possible

In one of the tense and crisis-torn meetings with black parents and leaders this week, I heard Lutheran minister Dr. Manas Buthelezi[2] say, "The victim of tomorrow is the person you meet today. Care for me today, not only when I become a dead body tomorrow."

In the story of the man who went down to Jericho and fell among brigands, the sin of the priest and the Levite was that their hearts never felt what their eyes saw. Too busy? Perhaps. Preoccupied with important things? Perhaps. For all we know they may have been going to a conference on street violence. It doesn't matter. What matters is that they didn't care when care was most desperately needed.

Right now, propagandists are looking for "agitators," and know-it-all authorities who ignored us when we tried to bring the crisis to their attention declare: "We didn't know." Wiser people are aghast at how deep are the wounds of black South Africans. But in it all, nobody cared enough until blood was shed and death came to visit. And we have seen that once violence breaks out, it becomes more difficult to care. Other forces like revenge and pillage, ruthless suppression, and blind rage begin to take control.

If anything good is to come out of any of this, it must surely be learned from the Samaritan who didn't just see; what he saw moved him to compassionate action.

We need to care while caring is possible.

Be Courageous with Love

Right now there is a powerful temptation for people to retreat into blocs, especially racial groups. That is what violence does—it polarizes. Suddenly *apartheid's* lines of racial separation, instituted, we were told, "to avoid friction," become the line of battle. In war, opposing forces wear different uniforms, and *apartheid* has made our uniform the color of our skin. Black and white confront each other in hostility.

There is little point in reminding you how often we have warned against this day. Let me rather go back to the Bible to remind you of God's firm answer to the false ideology of separation and division—Jesus Christ: *"For he is himself our peace. Gentiles and Jews [should we not read "black and white?"], he has made the two one, and in his own body of flesh and blood has broken down the enmity that stood like a dividing wall between them"* (Ephesians 2:14).

For many of us this issue of separation is a mere subject for debate. From the depths of our armchairs, we offer pompous and prejudiced opinion. Others have exploited every fear and racial superstition to defend an ungodly separation.

But others have lived the Gospel in the crucible of terrible violence.

I am both proud and shamed by some examples of faithfulness to this scripture that have come out of the carnage of Soweto. I think of the wife of one of our ministers in Soweto, who, even though surrounded by an angry crowd, gave sanctuary in her home to a white Afrikaner social worker who had been trapped in the midst of the violence.[3] She saved that woman's life at risk of her own. Hers was an act of courageous love, and—given the role of Afrikaans in all of this strife—also an act of magnanimous grace. She incarnated our conviction that in Christ the dividing wall cannot stand.

If anything is to be salvaged from this horror, we must be courageous with love. While the ruins still smolder, we must reach out our hands and ask and receive forgiveness.

The Blood Has Been Shed

At the height of the anti-Soviet revolt in Czechoslovakia, an exhausted young freedom fighter told a news reporter, "Some things are won only by the shedding of blood." That would seem to be the growing conviction of the youths whose blood has soaked Soweto's streets this week.

If this is so, what a tragic and bloody future lies ahead for us all. Such a future would fit Paul's description of the world the Ephesians once lived in: *"without hope and without God"* (Ephesians 2:12). Unless . . . Unless something has happened to change all that.

The Jews of biblical times too were convinced that there could be no forgiveness or liberation or peace without the shedding of blood. Does the Gospel of Jesus not tell us that all *has* changed because *in the death of Christ the blood has already been shed*? When Christ died on the cross, he died for the sins and brokenness of the world. The body of Jesus was broken so we could know God and find reconciliation with each other: *"you who once were far off have been brought near through the shedding of Christ's blood. For he is himself our peace"* (Ephesians 2:13-14) and: *"This was his purpose, to reconcile the two in a single body to God through the cross, on which he killed the enmity"* (Ephesians 2:16).

If we are to find a way through all this without much worse suffering and much more dying, this is the truth we need to enter far more fully than we have. God has already suffered to set us free from the very things that have brought bloodshed upon us now. When we take seriously the blood shed for all people, to break down every dividing wall, to reconcile every enemy, we will find hope to mend even the terrible brokenness that is upon us.

God help us to say to each other each day: "We need not, we should not, we dare not, shed each others' blood. It has happened already. Jesus did it for us. Whatever blood was needed for the mending of all our wrongs has been shed." Now is the time to live in the light of that sacrifice—and by the compassion and courageous love of the one who made it.

---

1. Vorster was about to leave for his first meeting with U.S. Secretary of State Henry Kissinger, and was convinced the June 16 demonstrations were aimed at sabotaging this foreign policy coup. He was utterly unmoved by the deaths beginnng to be reported. "You people started this nonsense; you can sort it out," was his comment to SACC President John Thorne.

2. Manas Buthelezi later became a Lutheran Bishop in Soweto and President of the SACC.

3. In all the months of youth activism following June 16, only three white persons died, all of them in the first hours of the strife. There were other examples of blacks providing sanctuary for white persons caught in the tumult. By contrast, at least five hundred black youths were killed by the police and security forces in 1976 alone.

4

These Things Are True

Presidential Address
South African Council of Churches National Conference,
Johannesburg, May 4, 1981

My task is to bear witness to the truth. For this was I born; for this I came into the world. (John 18:37)

How vast the resources of his power open to us who trust in him. They are measured by his strength and the might which he exercised in Christ when he raised him from the dead, when he enthroned him at his right hand in the heavenly realms, far above all government and authority, all power and dominion, and any title of sovereignty that can be named, not only in this age but in the age to come. (Ephesians 1:18-22)

When Church leaders, delegates, international guests, and media gathered in Johannesburg for the 1981 National Conference of the South African Council of Churches, the church/state conflict had swept us into a maelstrom of controversy and pain. A recent election—with only whites voting—cast a pall of depression over people committed to change. The triumphalism of white Republic celebrations rubbed salt into the wounds of the disenfranchised. Several bruising encounters with government left us in no doubt of their ruthlessness. The regime had acted against numbers of opponents, including SACC General Secretary, Bishop Desmond Tutu.

———

This National Conference meets in the glorious after-light of the Resurrection, where God declared Jesus to be Lord of all. Each day as we share the Eucharist we will be reminded that God has enthroned Jesus *"far above all government and authority, all power and dominion, and any title of sovereignty that can be named, not only in this age, but in the age to come."* Our God has *"put everything in subjection beneath his feet"* (Ephesians 1: 21-22).

This is the Christ who leads us. We are called, therefore, to live out of his Word, by his Spirit, under his cross. In repentance we will acknowledge that our sin is deep; in gratitude we will remember that we are saved only by his grace; in obedience we will answer the call to be his witnesses.

We meet also as members of a world family. Let our international visitors be welcomed as symbols of a vast brotherhood and sister-hood that transcends Jew and Greek, male and female, bond and free—and makes us all one in Christ Jesus. Let them be a reminder that the churches of this Council do not stand alone.

We meet as a sign of hope in a divided land. This Council is now the only forum in South Africa where all South Africans, black, white, and brown, can speak and listen to each other beyond the boundaries of denomination and race. In this gathering the privileged must shed their privilege and the voiceless must be heard. Here we acknowledge a common citizenship of one South Africa.

We come to seek the guidance of God for this common enterprise binding together some fifteen million people and to give account of our stewardship as a Council. We come to hear what the Spirit is saying to the Churches and to speak the words that God gives us to our nation and people.

Tonight I wish to speak some of those words.

We meet against the background of an election in which the very few of our people who have a genuine franchise—white South Africans—cast their votes. How I wish that we could speak of that election as an expression of the people's will, but we cannot. To the majority of South Africans, it is another ugly reminder of what has been denied them. It is simply a barometer of the views of the privileged. Instead of a celebration of democracy, it becomes a symbol of oppression.

We also meet against the background of the twentieth anniversary of South Africa's becoming a republic. How wonderful if this could have been an outpouring of loyalty by all South Africa's people. How wonderful if we could share the joy of being free men and women in a country that could hold its head high in the family of nations. Instead, even that which is good falls under the shadow of our deep national disease. As Christian leaders we must call, not for celebration, but for signs of repentance.

The degree to which people can celebrate these two events demonstrates the degree to which they have accepted a divided and balkanized South Africa. We who are the Body of Christ and who see all the people of this land as being of one family under God cannot. Both the republic festival and the white election are part of a great lie. This lie tells us that South Africa belongs to the few, and that the many who were here before the few came should be mere onlookers, receiving gratefully whatever bounty may be put in their direction and asking no questions.

Jesus said, *"My task is to bear witness to the truth. For this was I born; for this I came into the world"* (John 18:37). He also said, *"The truth will set you free"* (John 8:32).

As part of his body we too are obliged to witness to the truth. There can be no realistic grappling with the South African situation unless there is first a facing of South African truths; so while others dissect the election, and this false "republic festival" runs its course, here are some of the South African truths that we must declare today.

- The first is this: Every day that the policies of our government persist, South Africa moves twenty-four hours closer to conflagration. Every day that someone is arrested for a pass offense, detained without trial, turned out of their home, resettled against their will, separated from their wife or husband, denied access to work, informed that they are no longer citizens of the land of their birth[1]—every day that this happens, catastrophe is one day closer.
  That is the truth.

43

- A second is this: The greatest threat to peace and stability in this land is not a "total onslaught"[2] but the policy of *apartheid* and all that has flowed from it. There could be no total onslaught on a South Africa admired and respected in the Western world. There would be no fruitful soil for revolution in a South Africa at peace with itself. Those who envy South Africa's riches and strategic position would have little leverage if the young people of this land, black and white together, experienced it as a land of the free.
That is the truth.
- The third is this: In the long run, which is the only run that matters, white security based on *apartheid* is an illusion. Already white South Africans are an embattled people hiding behind high walls and burglar alarms and armed more heavily than any civilian population in the world. Every white male is now conscripted for two years in the face of what is at this stage only a "low intensity" border war. There comes a point when protecting one's privilege is such a full-time task that there is no time anymore to enjoy it. Slowly and inexorably white society is moving to that point.
That is the truth.
- Here is the fourth: *Apartheid* as a policy is doomed. It has been condemned in the councils of God, spurned by every democratic nation in the world, and is no longer believed in by the very government that gave it birth. What was once an ironclad ideology with the authority of sacred writ now lies in tatters. It stands revealed as a gigantic fraud with every single structure of government related to it distrusted and rejected by the people. Because *apartheid* is a lie, it relies on lies to support it and only the "blind and deaf" are fooled by it today.
That is the truth.
- Here is a fifth: The majority of the white population is still blind and deaf. In last week's white election, hardly a sixth of the 1.5 million white voters gave any sign of understanding these truths. While we are encouraged by the quarter million who were saying that some form of

power-sharing must come, we are horrified by those whose votes said in effect "We want change, but the change we want is a return to the Verwoerdian Dark Ages."[3] It is this kind of intransigence among whites that will send more young black people over the border for military training. Why should they have hope when just as some whites are beginning to see sense, a significant number are losing their senses entirely.

That is the truth.

It is against this background that our Council lives and witnesses today.

The obverse of these truths about white perceptions and white politics is a tale of dreadful black suffering on a greater scale than ever. Our divisional reports will speak of two million uprootings,[4] of continued unrest in schools, of more detentions without trial, of the growing detestation and bitterness of people forced to take out "homeland" citizenship, surrendering their South African birthright.

Our task is to continue to reveal these truths too for what they are. Call us unpatriotic if you will, but we want no part of a patriotism that hides the nation's disease when that disease is hurting people, hounding people, and breaking people each day. We believe the higher patriotism to be a determination so to expose the nerve ends of the truth that the conscience of even the most callous among us will be moved.

I invite the white people of this land to brush aside the fine-sounding phrases that clothe *apartheid* in respectability. Let whites open their eyes and learn the honesty of the child in the fable who trusted his own eyes rather than the stories spun by courtiers and cried, "The Emperor is naked!" Helmut Thielicke says that all compassion begins with the eyes, and we must pray for the eyes of Jesus.[5] The first step in caring is to see the man broken and beaten by the roadside. I would plead again as this Council has pleaded time without number: "See what *apartheid* and its offspring are doing to people! See and repent!" Until white people do, this Council of Churches must continue to witness to these truths.

I say to the Prime Minister who has been returned to power with what must be the biggest parliamentary majority in the Western world: "Hear what is being said at this conference. We have no dreams of power; we pose no political threat. In secular terms this Council is quite powerless. You can close us down tomorrow. Can you not believe then that the cry we raise comes not from some power strategy but from the heart? Can you not see that powerless as we are, our priests, ministers, and lay leaders are in touch with more grassroots people than your racially exclusive political party can ever be? Why would we bother if it were not for the fact that people are suffering?"

Our general secretary[6] has said that even now, at this late stage in the South African drama, a few bold measures in dismantling *apartheid* could change the entire scene, creating a new climate in which reason and mutual trust would replace frustration and violence. I have said to the prime minister[7] that our day does not call for politicians but for statesmen—leaders who can resist the short-term gain for the long-term good.

We bear witness to the truth, Mr. Prime Minister. It is a truth lived and discovered in countless homes and shanties across the land. We share it with you again from the platform of this conference because we believe that the grasping of this truth can set you and us together, free.

Now let me offer another perspective on the truths we must declare.

I have spoken of things political, *but the roots of politics lie always deeper than politics.* Amidst the turmoil of a nation wrestling with its chains, the pressures upon those who seek to bear witness to the truth are immense. Some pressures, such as the attempts to smear our general secretary, the removal of his passport, the death threats, are obvious and crude. But there are deeper and more subtle pressures that bring suspicion and division among us: A readiness to write someone off because his or her view of the struggle is different from my own; the quick labeling of people in destructive ways, as if that can really describe them; a willingness to trade the eternal truth of the Gospel for some fashionable ideology of change.

I have said that in any struggle there will be casualties, but it is tragic when the deepest pain comes at times not from the oppressive system but from a comrade in the struggle. Those of us who work for a more human, just, and generous South Africa need daily to inquire whether those desired qualities are alive in ourselves.

My father used to say: "Everything begins in theology and ends in politics." I believe him. I began this evening speaking of the Eucharist. This is where our roots must be. Whatever we have to say about this beloved country, whether of joy or pain—whatever word we offer to the wider South Africa—must find its origin here.

- Christ died for our sins—if the sins of South Africa are to be healed, I too must be touched by his forgiveness.
- Christ is alive—if his justice is to live in this land, his love must live in me.
- Christ will come again—he will ask not only what I achieved but also how I achieved it. Both questions will be important to him.

These things too are true. We witness to them when we come to this table.

Now let us lift up our hearts, for whatever dark passages this conference must explore, I pray with Paul:

> *that your inward eyes may be illumined, so that you may know what is the hope to which he calls you, . . . how vast the resources of his power open to us who trust in him. They are measured by his strength and the might which he exercised in Christ when he raised him from the dead, when he enthroned him at his right hand in the heavenly realms, far above all government and authority, all power and dominion, and any title of sovereignty that can be named, not only in this age but in the age to come.* (Ephesians 1:18-21)

---

1. All of these things were happening to millions of black South Africans in 1981. The *apartheid* regime had an arsenal of repressive laws designed to re-engineer the face of South Africa so that the majority of blacks would finally be "resettled" in a patchwork of artificial so-called "homelands," thus losing any right to be called South Africans.

2. "Total Onslaught" was the propaganda phrase used by the securocrats of P. W. Botha's regime to explain the world's hostility to them, the sanctions and divestment campaigns, and the growing guerrilla activities of the African National Congress. Their answer to it was what they called a "Total Strategy" that militarized much of South African life.

3. Difficult though it may be to believe, many white voters had opted for parties further right than the regime.

4. The forced removals policy ultimately uprooted 3.5 million people before P. W. Botha abandoned it in 1985.

5. Helmut Thielicke, "Sermon on the Parable of the Good Samaritan" in *The Waiting Father: Sermons on the Parables of Jesus* (New York: Harper, 1959).

6. Bishop (as he was then) Desmond Tutu, appointed in 1978.

7. P. W. Botha had succeeded Prime Minister Vorster, and the SACC leadership had met him in a notoriously unsuccessful encounter, followed almost immediately by the removal of Bishop Tutu's passport.

5

Hold Your Heads High —
Your Liberation Is Near!

Presidential Address
South African Council of Churches
National Conference, 1982

—When all this begins to happen, stand upright and hold your heads high, because your liberation is near. (Luke 21:28)

The storm was breaking about our heads. Confrontations, police beatings, and tear-gassing had taken place in churches around the country. President P. W. Botha[1] had announced a Commission of Inquiry into the affairs of the South African Council of Churches, and some of us would soon be interrogated in front of that tribunal. The Security Police were camping out in the SACC building, perusing its files and turning over every stone in our lives, hoping to find evidence with which to damn us.

It was important to give a word of hope.

—∭—

This is a decisive and troubled hour. For us, the years of crying out God's words of warning and calling for God's compassion and justice could be coming to a climax. The long shadow of state action stretches across this Council, and therefore over the Church. There are those who are hoping that out of all this will come some excuse to strike at the heart of Christian opposition to injustice and to silence its voice.

We watch the grand strategy of *apartheid* unfold like a horror movie before our eyes. The most radical dismemberment of any nation since the partition of India, the deliberate creation of unstable, unviable tribal dynasties where racism is exchanged for tribalism and white oppression gives way to black despotism.[2] Unable to dominate directly forever, the policy is now to divest this Republic of its sons and daughters by giving them away to whoever will take them.

We meet in an atmosphere charged with violence, in which the sons of white South Africans (and an increasing number of brown and black South Africans) are poured into the bottomless pit of war. Some of them are dying for a cause that cannot be defended and all of them surely know deep down that their victories are empty because their war is un-winnable. Others, born of the same soil and reared under the same sky, seek out targets for their time-bombs, regardless of who they may destroy. This is the land where a "quiet" June 16 sees the stones of anger fly and where churchmen are beaten in churchyards, their arms broken by police *sjamboks*.[3]

We live in an increasingly controlled society with information carefully screened for us. The ability to reveal truths to the nation is progressively limited, and it is now an offense to report the disappearance of a person into prison.

How can there be *Gospel*—Good News—at such a time as this?

Listen! Jesus spoke once of *"distress in the land and a terrible judgment upon the people,"* of nations standing *"helpless, not knowing where to turn,"* and also of things that have a familiar ring for this council: being dragged before kings and governors, being put in prison, being set upon and persecuted, being betrayed by parents, brothers, and friends (from Luke 21:12-28).

He spoke of wars and insurrections, of a nation under siege, and of people fainting with fear.

Then he said, *"When all this begins to happen, stand upright and hold your heads high, because your liberation is near"* (Luke 21:28).

That is astounding! The more so because he spoke these words when the road before him narrowed toward a cross, when the "chief priests and doctors of the law were trying to devise some means of doing away with him," and when Judas "began to look out for an opportunity to betray him" (Mark 17:11) without the people knowing.

After describing events that were fearsome and terrifying, the Son of God said: "Look up! The Kingdom of God is near! These things are like the buds on the fig tree—they are the promise of summer."

So today, this scripture gives us hope and good news. This truth flashes into our gloom; and in spite of the darkness, or even because of the darkness, we must hear the words: *"Your liberation is near!"*

Your Liberation Is Near
Because the False God Is Failing

When Jesus spoke these words, he was standing in the porch of Jerusalem's finest edifice—the Temple of Herod the Great. This magnificent, soaring building of marble and gold was the center and symbol of national life, and here a young country carpenter says: *"These things which you are gazing at—the time will come when not one stone of them will be left upon another; all will be thrown down"* (Luke 21:6).

The stones of South Africa's temple are tottering. The temple of *apartheid*, which once stood immovable and upon whose altars so many lives and hopes have been sacrificed, is shot through with fatal cracks. Its high priests of yesterday are remembered with embarrassment, and its devotees of today are an anachronism like the priests of Baal. The more they shout, the less happens.

Arthur Koestler and others once wrote a book called *The God That Failed*.[4] They were writing about Communism. But here is another failing god. In a few short years *apartheid* has been demythologized and discredited, stripped of its moral and religious buttresses and revealed for what it is—*just another tawdry means of exploiting people.*

After just four days in this country, Professor Kosuke Koyama of Union Theological Seminary said to me: "This policy is *pornographic* because it reduces precious human lives to a matter of skin and biology. It is *atheist* because its supreme criterion is something

51

for which we are not responsible and which we cannot change. All other things we can alter through repentance, forgiveness, and growth. This society judges people for the one thing they can do nothing about."[5]

Now, that which is so clearly evident after only four days to a person from a more normal world, is at last beginning to be seen (even if through a glass darkly) by those who have spent years of their lives worshiping at this temple.

When you see false gods failing, stand upright and hold your heads high because your liberation is near!

Know That the Victory Is Already Won

Christians live in the absurd belief that God's victory over sin has already happened. While others need the benefit of hindsight to identify the hinges upon which history turns, God gives God's people insight *in the midst of struggle*.

Historians of World War II will point to the Normandy landings and the battle of Stalingrad, and they will say: "There, in those battles the tide of war in Europe was turned." But if you had asked any soldier fighting to hold that beachhead or struggling to survive in the sewers of that city, he would have thought you were crazy. Yet now we know. Neither battle was the end of the fighting and suffering and dying, but at those two places the final result was assured.

In a far deeper way Jesus knew that when he mounted his cross, that day would prove evil to be only the second strongest force in the universe. How else could he say on the eve of his crucifixion: *"Courage! The victory is mine; I have conquered the world"* (John 16:33). So, if in the darkness of the cross the liberation of the world was won, I say that in these dark days the same certainty can be ours.

Does it matter in any *ultimate* sense that our lives are lived daily in the harsh light of hostile scrutiny? Does it matter in any *ultimate* sense that there are those who will not rest till they have exposed some or other weakness of ours (real or imagined) to trumpet to the world? The world did that to a perfect man, and we are far from perfect. Yet at the moment when he was most discredited, despised, and rejected, when he felt forsaken even by God—at that moment men beat their breasts in shame and the veil of the Temple was torn in two.

Is it a coincidence that just when some newspapers like to speak of this Council of Churches as "troubled" and "in crisis," 123 ministers of the church that is spoken of as not only supporting but having invented *apartheid* cry, "Enough! We can worship at that temple no longer!"[6]

When you see these things happening, know that at heart the battle is already won.

Now what do these words say to our life together as a conference, as a council, and as member Churches? I offer two thoughts.

Business as Usual

After these words and knowing the trials that lay before him, we read that Jesus' days *"were given to teaching in the temple; and then he would leave the city and spend the night on the hill called Olivet"* (Luke 21:37). Thus for the Savior, it was "business as usual," proclaiming God's word of judgment and mercy to all who would hear, and returning daily to his place of prayer and inward communion with his Father. Worship and engagement—engagement and worship: the quiet of God's presence and the intensity of God's struggle bound together in one life.

His instructions are to do the same:

> *Be on the alert, praying at all times for strength to pass safely through all these imminent troubles and to stand in the presence of the Son of Man.* (Luke 21:36)

That is surely where we must be in these coming days. We must live by that same rhythm. The world knows something of the work of this council through its actions, statements, and publications; God knows more of the worship of this council through its prayers, its worship, its breaking of bread. "Business as usual" for us is nothing ordinary. We must continue to give ourselves to God in worship and to people in costly engagement and service.

Live God's Future Now

If false gods are failing and if God's victory is assured, then even though this world has yet to acknowledge him, *we must live in his future now.* For the followers of Christ, he is already Lord—now!

- In a world of cruelty we know that compassion and caring will one day rule—so we will demonstrate them *now*.
- While this world bows to the love of power, we will cry, "No!"—we will live by the power of love *now*.
- While truth lies fallen in the streets, we will affirm that Jesus, who is the truth, is Lord—and we will live by his truth *now*.
- While people live comfortably with injustice we know that justice will one day rule—it must therefore be our standard *now*.
- While people continue to trust in military might, we know that the Prince of Peace is Lord—and we will cast out violence from our midst *now*.

That is what "business as usual" is all about for Christians. That is what the Christian hope is all about—not sentimental optimism but the insight that enables us even in the face of the darkest hour to know that Christ is Lord. Christian hope is living by God's future in the *now*.

I pray that we may be so filled with this quality of hope that when all this begins to happen, we will be able to stand upright and hold our heads high knowing that our liberation is near.

---

1. Prime Minister Botha had by this time, through a constitutional change, become Executive State President.

2. A tragic, but intended, consequence of *apartheid's* new ethnic "homelands" was the way they encouraged tribalism and relied on puppet black rulers to do the regime's work.

3. A leather whip or quirt.

4. Arthur Koestler et al., *The God That Failed* (Manchester, N. H.: Ayer, reprint of 1949 ed.).

5. Interview with Professor Koyama in my office earlier that year.

6. This refers to a statement by 123 ministers of the Dutch Reformed Churches, breaking with their denomination over its support of *apartheid*.

6

Here We Stand

*Introduction to testimony before the Commission of Inquiry
into the South African Council of Churches,
Pretoria, March 9, 1983*

State President P. W. Botha was now determined to put the South African Council of Churches out of business. With the liberation movements exiled, the Council was at this time the most prominent voice of resistance within South Africa's borders. Botha had announced a Commission of Inquiry, headed by a Supreme Court judge, to investigate the affairs of the SACC.

The primary motive for the investigation was to demonstrate that the SACC was either an active collaborator with, or a naive dupe of, the Liberation Movements and "Communist enemies" of South Africa who desired the overthrow of "Western Christian Civilization." An additional advantage to the government was the enormous diversion of energy required of the SACC to counter this attack.

At the public hearings in Pretoria, the nation's capital, Bishop Desmond Tutu[1] as General Secretary and I as President were the SACC's chief witnesses. After being permitted to make our opening statements, each of us was interrogated for more than twenty hours.

My statement before the commission, published as "Here We Stand," was a lengthy document. This was the introduction.

—⚭—

My Lord and members of the Eloff [2] Commission:

I come before you as one who has been placed by the South African Council of Churches (SACC) into the position of president of that Council, but first and foremost as a minister of the Gospel of Jesus Christ. I believe that there is no greater privilege and responsibility than that of ministering the Word of God and shepherding God's people. Because whatever position a minister may hold, there is none more ultimately binding than the vows of ordination; it is as a simple minister of the Gospel that I shall speak.

Equally, because of these convictions, I believe that I am first, always, and last a servant of Christ. His task must be my task, his calling must be my calling, his way must be my way. Any other loyalty, whether to nation, family, people, or party, must be subservient to this and must be looked at in its light. I know that on the Day of Judgment, all that I have lived for will be tested against this measure.

Neither I nor anyone else can live up to this high calling, but in my theology the word *grace* has a special place. When I fail, God in God's infinite grace offers me forgiveness and calls me again to follow God's Son. That is the wonder, the surprise, and the supreme "improbability" of the Good News. Christ is God's sign of forgiveness, of new beginnings, and of new life for those who fail. The only hope for me or for any person is to live in this consciousness of being forgiven and accepted, and in the power and joy and freedom that this forgiveness brings to live again for him.

I believe very sincerely in our Lord's promise that when we know the truth, "the truth will make us free." In responding to some of the hard and cruel things that have been said about the SACC, I will try to use the truth as I have seen and understood it. If there is at times some anger in what I say, it will be not out of a sense of personal grievance, but rather because I believe that in this commission, the truth has been violated, the church misrepresented, and our Lord grieved.

It has been a strange experience sitting here while others have painted a picture of the SACC so different from my own experience. I have listened with a sense of unreality as some witnesses particularly have described this body to which I belong and its history as part of a web of intrigue, serving dark intentions and designed to bring chaos to our land.

The SACC that I know is a different one. It is an attempt against the heavy odds of prejudice, the captivity of our past, and the oppression of our present, to be a light on a hill and a transforming leaven in a land of division, hopelessness, and fear.

The greatest weakness of the case brought against us is that history has been read with one eye closed. As I have listened to evidence given, I have heard much of the "total onslaught," a political slogan which has been given an almost biblical authority. I have heard of the strategies of international Communism and its surrogates. I have heard of how we, the SACC, have become allies or at least willing dupes of these forces.

But I have waited in vain to hear one word about the other makers of South African history in our time: the inventors of *apartheid*. It is as if the history of South Africa and that of the SACC in this country has unfolded in a benevolent vacuum. Nowhere in these analyses of our role in South Africa is there any recognition of the pivotal part played by successive South African *apartheid* governments since 1948.

It may be argued that it is the SACC and not the South African government that is under examination. I submit, however, that to examine our role without taking proper cognizance of the main context in which it has been lived out, is as meaningless as, say, trying to understand the life of Abraham Lincoln without mentioning slavery, or to study the theology of Dietrich Bonhoeffer without mentioning Nazism.

From evidence given thus far, a stranger to South Africa would be forgiven for assuming that the land in which the SACC witnesses was an idyllic place governed by the most passive government in the world and surrounded by enemies with evil intent.

I wish to paint another picture. Who we are, and what we have tried to do, arises out of two great realities:

> The first is our understanding of the Scriptures and the Gospel of which we are messengers. Bishop Tutu has made this point with great power.
>
> The second is the context of our *apartheid* society. We have been called to witness to Christ in a society stained by a great corporate sin, for that is what the *apartheid* doctrine is.
> - It is a sin against God the Father who wills that all should be God's sons and daughters;
> - It is a sin against God the Son who died to reconcile all people to God and to each other;
> - It is a sin against the Holy Spirit who makes us all one in the unity of the spirit in the bonds of peace.

If you accept that *apartheid* can be right anywhere, you say that Christ's work of reconciliation on the cross has failed everywhere. Accept that *apartheid* can be valid anywhere, and you say that the divisions of humanity are in the end more powerful than the saving work of Jesus, of whom Saint Paul said:

> *For he is himself our peace. Gentiles and Jews, he has made the two one, and in his own body of flesh and blood has broken down the enmity which stood like a dividing wall between them; for he annulled the law with its rules and regulations, so as to create out of the two a single new humanity in himself, thereby making peace. This was his purpose, to reconcile the two in a single body to God through the cross, on which he killed the enmity.* (Ephesians 2:14-16)

I want to declare to this commission that the key to our life as a Council of Christian Churches will be found in these two realities: seeking to be bearers of the biblical message of the Kingdom of God in a society dominated by this great denial of the Kingdom.

There is not one of us who relishes this task. Bishop Tutu has often enough spoken of his wish to be riding ponies in the mountains of Lesotho, conducting confirmations. I would love nothing more than to spend all my time preaching, serving the people of my congregation, and helping them to demonstrate the caring of

Christ in the center of Johannesburg. It is out of a sense of deep obedience to the Gospel and concern for the pain of our land that we do what we do.

That is why it has at times been difficult to listen to what has been said about us here. It is part of the Christian's burden to be gripped by what Bishop Tutu has called the "Divine Intention" and to know that you are an unprofitable servant whose obedience to that intention has often failed. That is a fact that we recognize and must live with, trusting in God's forgiveness.

But when the *intention itself* is misrepresented, its motives are questioned, and other less worthy intentions and motives are attributed to us, we must say No—that is a lie which cannot go unchallenged.

It has been a special privilege for me to be part of the life of the SACC. I see its achievements and its failures, and above all I have lived with its dilemmas; and I say without doubt that those dilemmas arise supremely out of seeking to be a messenger and model of God's intention for South Africa. While others have lived in compartments of language and race, and therefore as prisoners of South Africa's history, the Council and its member churches work toward God's future for South Africa *and try to live that future now.* In doing so we have discovered much of the pain and joy of togetherness, and we know that God wants that experience for all of South Africa's people.

The pain of our togetherness is real. My wife works at the SACC.[3] She has two sons in National Service, and she works with women whose sons are somewhere on the other side. She has learned to cry with them and they with her. That is part of the pain of togetherness.

But the joy outweighs it. *"There is a special joy,"* says Jesus *"for those who hunger and thirst to see right prevail. They shall be satisfied."* Even when we fail, or others misrepresent us, even living as we do at the intersection of so much of South Africa's agony, we have learned to rejoice.

We cherish both this pain and this joy for all South Africans. In all that we have done, we have said and will continue to say:

The road that South Africa walks is a road that leads ever more deeply into division and destruction. It is a road away from God. Please walk down that road no longer. We call all South Africans to a new and higher road. It is a far better thing to pay the price, however high, of seeking God's intention of unity for us all. It is this road that the SACC believes it has been called to walk. If this road should lead to a Jerusalem and a cross, so be it. It is the road that Jesus walked, and beyond the cross there is always an Easter.

---

1. His powerful biblical and theological defense of the witness of the SACC was published under the title "The Divine Intention" (SACC, Braamfontein, 1982).

2. Named for Mr. Justice Eloff, the Supreme Court judge who chaired the Commission.

3. Elizabeth was secretary to three general secretaries of the SACC, the last being Bishop Tutu.

7

They Have Damned Their Souls

Memorial Service for Jeanette and Katryn Schoon,
Central Methodist Church, July 3, 1984

> *Do not be surprised if the world hates you. We for our part have*
> *passed over from death to life; this we know, because we love our*
> *brothers. The man who does not love is still in the realm of death,*
> *for everyone who hates his brother is a murderer, and no*
> *murderer, as you know, has eternal life dwelling in him.*
> *(1 John 3:13-16)*

Jeanette Schoon (thirty-five) was married to African National Congress activist Marius Schoon, living in exile in Botswana. She and their young daughter, Katryn, were killed by a parcel bomb, organized (we now know) by Major Craig Williamson, a notorious Security Police operative. Marius and their other child, Fritz, were not there when the parcel was opened.

At the request of Jeanette's parents, Jack and Joyce Curtis, the memorial service took place at Central Methodist

Mission. Neither Marius or Fritz could attend—they had to remain in exile until liberation.

For me, this was one of those times when the ability to give hope dried up. After spending time with Jenny's broken parents, there was nothing left. This brief address, one of a number that day, expresses more anger on behalf of the grieving family, and terrible frustration at the dark forces who could lash out with such impunity, than it does hope or comfort.

Since then, Williamson has applied for and received amnesty through the Truth and Reconciliation Commission. Marius Schoon was one of the most prominent victims to oppose the amnesty provisions for former *apartheid* human rights violators. Who would not have some sympathy for his stand? Williamson's amnesty has tested my commitment to the Truth and Reconciliation process more than any other, but that is in the nature of this remarkable endeavor. To deal with the genuine wounds of our past, truth and reconciliation will always ask more of us than we can easily forgive—that is what it is about.

—ɷ—

It is a truism that society crucifies not only those who fall below its standards but those who rise above them. Jenny was one such. Leaving this land was part of her deep rejection of *apartheid* and all it stood for.

Jenny had suffered detention without trial for sixty-eight days, with all that means in torture and interrogation. She and Marius were both banned[1] persons when they first met. They were married by the Reverend Theo Kotze in Mary Taylor's[2] flat. Hours later they left together on a "honeymoon picnic," carrying some odd equipment, including a flashlight and compass. The next day they were across the border in Botswana.

Ironically, Jenny had recently reassured her mother that she was out of danger. She was "not involved" and no longer belonged to any movement because, she said, "one of us must be free of that for the children's sake."

Those who sent the bomb had little interest in such scruples.

The Bible speaks of the fallenness of humanity. It speaks about people who "love darkness because their deeds are evil." Today we are reminded again of the depths of evil to which human beings can sink.

We can only speculate on her murderer or murderers; but whoever they are, *I want them to know that right now, they have damned their own souls.*

Their action exposes to the light the utter senselessness of all political violence. The moral bankruptcy, the blind, unfeeling callousness that masquerades behind all attempts at justification. All such acts, whoever perpetrates them and for whatever cause, rise out of the same cesspool; they lie under the same condemnation and will receive the same judgement.

An inhuman system produces inhuman consequences, and the reason why Jenny and Katryn, Marius and Fritz, are not living quietly and happily in one of the suburbs of this city, must be traced back directly to the kind of society we have made. This is a fruit of *apartheid*. Much of Jenny's life had been given to resisting it. Now her life has been taken by it. This is another tragic, murderous chapter in the story of South Africa's pain.

She is another sacrifice on the altar of *apartheid*.

God forgive us.

---

1. Banning made a nonperson out of you. It denied participation in named activities, attendance at gatherings, entry to numerous places, publication of anything you said or wrote. You simply ceased to impact your world.

2. Both were activists. Theo Kotze, a Methodist minister working for the Christian Institute, went into exile after being served a banning order.

8

Celebrate With Me!

Witness to the World Methodist Council,
Kenyatta Center,
Nairobi, 1986

Here and now I will do a new thing; this moment it will break
from the bud. Can you not perceive it? (Isaiah 43:19)

When the delegates to the World Methodist Council met for the first time on African soil in 1986, the struggle against *apartheid* and the stand of the South African Church was the focus of attention. The Right Reverend Desmond Tutu, soon to be Anglican Archbishop of Cape Town, was a keynote speaker and joined us in the march of witness through Nairobi. The Reverend Abel Hendricks, a former leader of the Methodist Church of Southern Africa, was awarded the World Methodist Peace Prize. This witness was given at one of the plenary sessions.

—⁂—

Yesterday the good citizens of Nairobi saw a stirring sight—the spiritual descendants of John Wesley from seventy nations, marching behind their banners, bearing witness to Jesus through the streets of this city.

For the most part the procession was conducted with the dignity and decorum proper for Christians on a Sunday afternoon, *but right at the tail end something different was happening.* A dancing, singing, shouting, sweating group of South Africans, swelled by South African refugees living here in exile, were having themselves a party! We were even joined by the Anglican Archbishop-elect of Cape Town—reaching down into his roots and finding his Methodist baptism and upbringing. And among the black South Africans, swaying to the rhythms of Africa, were white South Africans discovering to their surprise that they too had ball-bearings in their hips. Blacks and whites together—from South Africa—celebrating!

Afterwards, as I was mopping the sweat and trying to recover my dignity, someone asked me a question: "How is it possible?—after all we have heard and all we know—the agony, the discord, the violence, and the hate—how can you celebrate like that? How can such joy spring from such pain?"

Let me try to answer that question. I'm here to give a testimony—to share Good News.

Celebrate with Me That God Is Alive in the Furnace of *Apartheid*

If you want to know whether God is alive, don't go to the places of comfort and ease. Inquire rather in those places where the fire of testing burns most fiercely. Living in the furnace of *apartheid* forges a unique experience of God. It melts away cheap piety, until all that is left is something you know is *real*—some*one* you know is real. You discover that with you in that furnace is another, *"whose form is like that of the Son of God."*

I have two testimonies—every white South African must have *two* testimonies. The first is one that so many of you know well: Jesus told a story once that leaped across two thousand years and lodged in my heart, of a son and a father, a far country and a family home. That story explored the geography of my soul. It told me I was a long way from home, but it also told me that there was someone back there scanning the road each day—and that if I turned for home, I would find the extravagant love of a Father running to meet me. I believed the storyteller. I made that journey and found through my tears that he had kept his word. Since that moment the journey has had to be made not once but many times, and I've come to discover something about myself. There is the self I know and despair of—the *self*-truth, if you like. The self-truth says, "Make me a hired servant—I have sinned." But there is another truth about me in the heart of God, and the *God*-truth says, "this my son was lost and is found again—was dead and is alive!" Let's have a party!

Every white South African, however, needs a *second* conversion—like the blind man who needed to be touched again by Jesus. The first time, you remember, Jesus asked, "Can you see?" The man peered out of his newly opened eyes and said, "Yes—I think so—I can see people—they look like trees walking." And Jesus said, "Go and wash your eyes again!" (from Mark 8:22-26). The curse of South Africa is that there are so many Christians who name the name of Jesus, claiming to have been touched by him, *who look out of eyes blinded by three hundred years of power and privilege—and see walking trees instead of people.*

I give thanks tonight for those—my own father, some amazing black Christians, friends who are here today—who told me to wash again. They are still helping me deal with the consequences in my soul of the whiteness of my skin.

I give thanks that God is alive in the furnace of *apartheid.*

I Want You to Celebrate with Me That Jesus Breaks the Walls!

South Africa needs evangelism, but in South Africa evangelical conversion is never to Jesus alone. In South Africa when we sing "Come into my heart, Lord Jesus," he says, *"Only if I can bring my friends."*

I celebrate tonight the way in which that experience is happening in the lives of many white South Africans. That dancing and singing you saw yesterday is the promise of the new South Africa. We are not some pathetic remnant trying vainly to recall a lost past; we are heralds of God's new future! God says:

> *Here and now I will do a new thing; this moment it will break from the bud. Can you not perceive it?* (Isaiah 43:19)

Some think it foolish to talk of evangelism in a country about to tear itself to pieces, but the spiritual descendants of John Wesley know differently. If the only thing that can save South Africa is political repentance—*surrender of power and privilege*—then only those persons who have known the liberating power of the cross have any message for the whites of South Africa. Only such persons can speak with confidence *of the freedom that comes through letting go.* If the grace of God can conquer the pride and prejudice of a sinful heart, that same God can overcome the power and privilege that holds South Africa captive.

So the Jesus we preach is a Jesus who breaks the walls, who has destroyed the middle wall of partition, and who has brought together black and white, making them one in his single body on the cross (Ephesians 2:14). The evangelism we offer preaches Christ and his burning passion for the world. We lift the cross, not as a way of escape *but as that place where at his invitation we are nailed to his passion and where he nails us to our neighbour*—that is the evangelism I speak of.

At one of our services at the Central Methodist Mission in Johannesburg, there came and knelt at the Communion rail a young white man. In counseling afterward, he told me his story and shared a crippling burden of guilt. He had been a policeman in Soweto during the uprising of 1976.[1] He had participated in the dreadful brutality that has become familiar to you on your television screens across the world. Now the Gospel had touched him and had searched his soul. He wanted to be clean. Some months later we received him into membership. He knelt again at that same Communion rail to be confirmed, the hands of the president of our church reached out to be laid on his head—and those hands were black hands. The voice that confirmed him in his pardon, in his forgiveness, in his acceptance, spoke in the rhythms of black Africa.

The walls were down. Only Jesus can do that!

Celebrate with Me the Indestructible Liberty of the Sons and Daughters of God

For an all too brief twenty-four months I ministered as a chaplain to Robben Island, that bleak prison island off Cape Town which many call the University of the New South Africa. There I ministered to Nelson Mandela in his cell block and to Robert Sobukwe in the house where he was kept for many years in total isolation.

Both were Methodists—one the leader of the African National Congress, the other the leader of the Pan African Congress.

Robert Sobukwe is now dead.[2] Let me tell you about him. From the front door of his house you could see across the eleven miles of sea to the city of Cape Town, with its graceful Parliament buildings. I asked him what it felt like to see freedom so near, yet so far. Quietly he answered, *"Peter, they are the prisoners—they are the ones who need to be set free."*

Let me speak to you of another prisoner dressed in canvas shorts and shoes cut out of motor car tires, who came up to me one day and asked for Holy Communion, who I now know suffered terrible degradation in the years he spent on that island. It would be wrong for me to say more about things I have never suffered—especially when he himself almost never mentions it. Where is he today? Is he broken—has he lost the dream? No, on Saturday, when Bishop Cannon called for the voice of the South African Methodists to be heard, it was he who mounted this podium as secretary of our conference and spoke for us all.[3]

Oh, God is real in that furnace—can you doubt that liberation will come to my land?

Celebrate with Me the Church as the Community of Hope

Last month Dr. Dudley Weeks, who is a Washington-based conflict resolution expert, sat in my office and said: "I don't have a religious background, but I have traveled the trouble spots of the world and I have never seen a nation where the Church has such a strategic, crucial role. In South Africa the Church is the only hope." I believe that.

The Church has wrestled with *apartheid* from the day of its birth. It was only when the Church broke with racism and when God, with an exquisite sense of humor, gave Paul the Pharisee a Gentile congregation for his first pastoral charge—it was only then that the disciples got the name "Christians" (Acts 11). The first ever Council of the Church—and its first ever doctrinal pronouncement—was really about *apartheid*, when a group of Jewish Christians said to Gentiles, "You can join us, but only if you become like us first," and the Church decided adamantly against that form of exclusion (Acts 15).

Ever since then this so fallibly human, mysteriously divine community we call the Church, has been the community of hope.

Tension between church and state is nothing new. It began with the Incarnation, when Herod decided that there was room for only one king in Judea and Jesus became a refugee.

The Methodist Church in Southern Africa is not neutral in the conflict with Caesar; *we are committed to the downfall of* apartheid *and the liberation of its victims.* Call us unpatriotic if you will—we want no part of a patriotism that defends the indefensible. We live by a higher patriotism that needs to expose the nerve-ends of our people's and our nation's pain and say, "Look at it and repent." I love South Africa too passionately to let her die of her disease when a cure is available. We will not put the Church at the disposal of the State.

The Church is the community of hope, not only in the macro sense but also for individual lives, in the challenge that an inclusive community brings to a divided society. Even in the pain and horror of today's South Africa, our God still makes this point—and sometimes does so in quite a naughty way!

Let me tell you a story. Even in the pain and horror of what's happening there we can laugh.

There is in this hall, somewhere, Ike Moloabi,[4] who was in prison a few weeks ago. There were still some loopholes in the State of Emergency regulations, so I, together with another minister, was able to visit him. They put us in a corner with an Afrikaner prison officer to monitor our conversation. We could say little to each other, but I did have in my pockets some bread and a small chalice and some communion wine, so we prepared to celebrate the Eucharist.

Now Methodists have an open table, so naturally I invited the prison officer to join us and have communion with us, and after some hesitation, he accepted. And Methodists always serve the least of Christ's brothers and sisters first, don't we? So I passed the cup to Ike, and he drank. And Methodists would never take communion before offering it to the stranger in their midst, so the cup was naturally passed next to the prison officer. Now this white Afrikaner had a dilemma. He realized that if he wanted to receive the means of God's grace, he would have to place his lips for the first time in his life on a cup from which a black man had just drunk. You have to come from South Africa to know what that means. After a long pause, he took the cup and he drank—and for the first time, I saw the hint of a smile on Ike's face.

Then, at the end, I confess that I introduced a variation in the liturgy. I said, "We Methodists always hold hands when we say the grace." I asked the Lord to help me keep a straight face as prison officer and prisoner held hands and I recited the ancient words of benediction.

I wish I could report a miraculous release, but I cannot. Ike was kept some days longer. But there was another kind of miracle: The power-equation between this prison guard and Ike could not remain the same.

Do you see? Do you remember Paul's words to the Philippians?

> *Friends, I want you to understand that the work of the Gospel has been helped on, rather than hindered, by this business of mine. My imprisonment in Christ's cause has become common knowledge to all at headquarters . . . and it has given confidence to most of our fellow-Christians to speak the word of God fearlessly and with extraordinary courage.* (Philippians 1:12-14)

The Church is the community of hope in South Africa.

Celebrate with Me That *Apartheid* is Doomed

Because God is alive in the furnace; because Jesus breaks the walls; because Jesus gives a liberty that none can take away; because his Church will be kept faithful to hope . . . let me now witness from this platform of World Methodism to those in the places of power in Pretoria.

Let me witness to that government which, deaf to Christian conscience and blind to human consequence, has taken the dark impulses that lie in every heart and written them into the law of the land—bringing the Beloved Country to disaster.

Let me say to Mr. Botha,[5] "*Apartheid* is doomed!" It has been condemned in the Councils of God, rejected by every nation on the planet and is no longer believed in by the very people who gave it birth. *Apartheid* is the god that has failed.

Let me say to Mr. Botha, "Let not one more sacred life be offered at *apartheid's* blood-stained altar. In the name of the one true God, the God of Abraham, Isaac, and Jacob, the God and Father of our

Lord Jesus Christ—stop! Stop this evil thing! Open the prison doors! Call the exiles home! Burn the population register with its pornographic classifications of God's children by the color of their skin! Do it now! For as sure as God lives and as Jesus is Lord, you will have to do it in the end!"

On the altar in my church in Johannesburg, there stands a candle. It's not an ordinary candle. It is surrounded by a coil of barbed wire—the Amnesty Candle. Every Sunday there comes a moment when we pray for South Africa, when we read the names of those we know in prison, when we commit ourselves again to justice. Then we light the candle, and suddenly, in the middle of those cruel, imprisoning coils, a flame begins to burn.

We remember the words of John's Gospel: *"The light shines on in the dark, and the darkness has never mastered it"* (John 1:5).

I have tried to share some of that light with you tonight.

Then we pray the prayer for Africa. I ask you to bow your heads and pray it with me now:

> God bless Africa
> Guard her children,
> Guide her leaders,
> And give her peace.
> Through Jesus Christ our Lord.
> Amen.[6]

---

1. This young man was a conscript. The June 16, 1976, uprising by school children is referred to in greater detail in chapter 3.

2. Sobukwe was released from Robben Island after nine years, suffering from terminal cancer. He died in Kimberley in 1978.

3. The Reverend Stanley Mogoba, when a school teacher, had been imprisoned on Robben Island for Pan Africanist Congress activities. He later entered the ordained ministry and taught at the Federal Theological Seminary. By 1986 he was secretary of the conference of the Methodist Church of Southern Africa. Soon he was to be elected its presiding bishop.

4. The Reverend Ike Moloabi was our minister in *Ikageng*, the black township outside the conservative Afrikaner town of Potchefstroom, one hundred kilometers from Johannesburg. He was picked up by the Security Police in the early hours of June 20, 1986, and detained without trial under the Emergency Regulations. Normally we would have been automatically refused access to him, but someone was careless.

5. State president, P. W. Botha.

6. This widely used prayer was composed by Bishop Trevor Huddleston, Community of the Resurrection.

9

Finding Our Strength in God

Nationwide Radio Broadcast, Central Methodist Church
Johannesburg, June 22, 1986

Find your strength in the Lord, in his mighty power.
(Ephesians 6:10)

The year 1986 saw increasingly violent repression and increasingly aggressive resistance. South Africa's people were trapped between the ruthlessness of the government's state of emergency and the growing violence of the grassroots campaign "to make South Africa ungovernable." Hundreds had been taken into prison without trial. It was these prisoners of conscience I had most in mind as I preached.

Fierce debates within resistance circles revolved around the degree to which we should participate in, or boycott, institutions, serving the *apartheid* state. The South African Broadcasting Corporation (SABC), known to us as "His Master's Voice," controlled all radio and television in South Africa and was a servile instrument of the regime.

Nevertheless, it did make time available for broadcasts of church services, and in spite of a number of running battles with the SABC on other matters, I determined to continue broadcasting as long as there was no interference with the content of our services or the sermons. One reason for doing this was that the listening audience for these services was larger than for any other SABC program, offering a national platform to speak some scriptural truth into the situation. Another was a letter from Nelson Mandela, indicating that he and other political prisoners, whose only contact with the outside world was through the radio, valued these broadcasts and were encouraged by them.

—⚍—

Tonight, we worship in an atmosphere dark with fear and foreboding. All people of Christian conscience who long for peace and justice will know that South Africa stands in its deepest crisis. Perhaps even those who have disregarded the warnings of the prophets will at last recognize that God's judgment is upon us, and upon all our ways.

Many, many people are suffering at this time for conscience' sake, and my prayers go out to them. In asking God what I should say in this broadcast my thoughts were led to another prisoner of conscience, waiting in his cell for execution. His name was Paul, the great Christian evangelist. He was in chains too. He had every right to be hopeless; yet surprisingly, instead of thinking of himself as a prisoner, he called himself an ambassador—in chains! He had a message to deliver on behalf of God, and his deepest concern was that his message would get through. So he asked his friends to pray for him: *"Pray that I may speak of it boldly, as it is my duty to speak"* (Ephesians 6:20).

His message did get through. For two thousand years followers of Jesus have had their hearts encouraged and their wills reinforced by Paul's words in Ephesians, chapter 6, from verse 10. He starts by calling us to turn to God: *"Find your strength in the Lord, in his mighty power!"*

Then he goes on to design a suit of armor for those facing the power of evil. I want us to listen carefully.

When Your Strength Is in God, No One Is Your Enemy

In times like these there is a dangerous tendency to identify people as the enemies that need to be resisted and destroyed.

Down the centuries when things have gone wrong, there has always been a search for scapegoats—someone, or some group upon whom to lay the blame. "There they are. . . . they are the cause of our trouble!" Hitler pointed to the Jews, Idi Amin blamed the Indian traders of Uganda. Here in South Africa, depending on who you are, it's the whites, the blacks, the ANC or AWB.[1]

The apostle Paul knew all about this thirst for an enemy. There was a time when he ran around imprisoning every Christian he could find. Now here he was in prison, *because he was a Christian!* Christians had been identified as enemies of the state, threatening the security of Rome.

But, from his prison chains, Paul warns against being taken in by "enemy" talk. "Our fight is not against human foes," he says. "The true enemy who can destroy us all is not made of flesh and blood. You're looking in the wrong place."

"Our fight," he says, "is against cosmic powers, against the authorities and potentates of this dark world, against the superhuman forces of evil in the heavens."

Let me tell you of the cosmic powers—the superhuman forces of evil that have brought us to this state of emergency:

> Fear is one of them;
>   racial hate is another,
>   pride and arrogance too,
>   the refusal to share,
>   and the insane trust in force.

These are the true enemies of South Africa, the forces that have driven this country on a reckless course to division and disaster. You don't fight these forces with guns and emergency regulations, or by locking people up. These enemies are within our souls, and we need to be liberated from them.

This is something only the changing power of God can do; but when that power takes hold, miracles can happen. People who thought they were enemies see the face of Christ in each other's faces.

I learned this in a very profound way when in 1981 I traveled to Dresden, in Communist East Germany. I was attending the first meeting of the World Council of Churches to be held in the Eastern bloc. In order to get to Dresden from Berlin, you passed first through "Checkpoint Charlie," into East Berlin, and then you had to travel some three hundred kilometers, through what was known as the *"sperrgebied"*—the forbidden zone. Here the military forces of the East were deployed for the attack from the West that, in their minds, could come at any time. Along that road there was just one stop, a small filling station and a place where you could get out of the car and eat some sandwiches. There were very heavy penalties for stopping a vehicle anywhere else. As you drove, you caught occasional glimpses through the forests of tanks and artillery pieces, of observation posts and the other paraphernalia of war. We were in "enemy" territory.

Then we got to Dresden. It was a spooky feeling as our convoy of buses moved in the dusk down to the square. We could see people in the gloom, but they were being held back by the political police, the *Volkspolizei*. As we disembarked there was total silence, a silence populated by suspicion and fear. We moved into the great *Kreutzkirche*, the Church of the Cross, which only that year had been renovated and partially rebuilt from World War II bomb damage. It was elliptical in shape with three balconies, one above the other, all empty. A great cross was marked in the ceiling above that, the full length of the sanctuary.

As we took our seats on the ground floor, feeling uneasy and insecure, we heard the shuffling of hundreds of shoes as the people of Dresden began moving into the galleries. They had been permitted to come and watch this service. That shuffling was the only sound there was.

And then the service began. The organ thundered out with Luther's "A Mighty Fortress Is Our God"; and as we stood to sing, something happened. We felt what seemed to be like raindrops falling on us. We looked up, and there were just hundreds of hands reaching over the balconies to us, each waving a white handkerchief. The people were smiling and weeping at the same time, and their tears were falling on us. Our "enemies" were welcoming us; and in the days that followed, they continued to do so, in spite of all their ideological rulers' attempts to stop them.

No person is your enemy!

When Your Strength Is in God, Christ Is Lord

If people are not our enemy, if the forces we are up against are more superhuman than human, what must we do? Paul says we must find our strength in the Lord and in his mighty power.

But what can a crucified carpenter do? How could this man Paul, locked in prison like so many in our land today, be so sure? Paul knew something that every lover of justice must hold on to in a time like this.

Christ is Lord!

In the first chapter of this letter he says that God has enthroned Christ at his right hand, *"far above all government and authority, all power and dominion and any title of sovereignty that can be named."*

"God put everything in subjection beneath Jesus' feet."

When Jesus mounted his cross, that day proved that evil was only the second strongest force in the universe.

That's what Paul meant, and that's how he was sure!

This is the certainty that has held Christians firm in their witness against impossible odds. This is the certainty for which Paul said, *"I am an ambassador in chains"*; and although he spoke from a prison cell and was soon to die, he knew!

This is the certainty that took Martin Niemöller to prison in Hitler's Germany. When he came to trial charged with disobeying Hitler, this is the certainty that led him to declare: *"The Lord is my Fuhrer."*

Let those who perpetrate injustice and hurt and violence on any of God's children know that Christ is Lord and he will have the last word. The forces ranged against those who witness for love, for peace, and for justice may be powerful; but the power of the risen Lord will overcome them.

Alan Walker writes of the time when he first stood in the arena of Rome's Coliseum, wondering how Christians in the first century found the courage to face wild beasts while the crowds screamed for their blood. Then, later he went into the catacombs—sixteen miles of tunnels under the city—and saw the simple stone altars where these same Christians had worshiped. Here was the key to their courage.[2]

Find your strength in the Lord, and in his mighty power.

When Your Strength Is in God, You Wear God's Armor

It is amazing to me that after centuries of failure, humanity still trusts in military might and the discredited way of war and violence. Whether used to crush liberty or to fight for it, the weapons of war bring no permanent solution.

Paul urges us to take up God's armor, the belt of truth, the coat of integrity, and the shoes of peace. He tells us to carry the shield of faith and wear salvation for a helmet, wielding only God's word for a sword.

- I wonder—is it too late for South Africa to change her weaponry?
- To put our faith in truth instead of propaganda,
- To find a new integrity and live by our declared convictions,
- To truly seek peace—not the uneasy brooding silence of repression but the shalom of God, the peace that is only reached through the gates of justice?
- Have we faith enough to believe that if we do God's will and practice justice and mercy, God will heal our land?
- Are we sure of our salvation? Have we repented and found forgiveness? Only such people are free to be different.
- Can we cast aside fear and take into our hearts instead the promises of God, bearing God's word, Jesus Christ, as our only weapon?

Don't say it is impossible! By saying that, you sentence this land to death. Rather say, "We have tried the outworn ways of cruelty, and they have brought us to the edge of the abyss. Let us turn away from force and repression and lies. Let God do a new thing among us soon . . . now!"

Let there be an end to our seeking for enemies to hate and fear. Let us rather admit that hate and fear are the real enemies who bind us. Let us confess Christ as Lord and hold ourselves and our government accountable to him.

If we let God do these things among us, then hope can be born again because South Africa can be born again.

---

1. "Afrikaanse Weerstand Beweging," or Afrikaner Resistance Movement, the extreme right-wing neo-Nazis.

2. Alan Walker, *My Faith Is Enough* (General Conference Literature and Publications Committee of the Methodist Church of Australasia), p. 56.

10

The Power of Faithful Suffering

*Central Methodist Mission, 1990,
and various pulpits in the United States of America*

*From that time Jesus began to make it clear to his disciples that
he had to go to Jerusalem, and there to suffer much.*
(Matthew 16:21)

*My dear friends, do not be bewildered by the fiery ordeal that is
upon you, as though it were something extraordinary. It gives
you a share in Christ's sufferings, and that is cause for joy.*
(1 Peter 4:12-13)

One cannot journey from Africa to the United States of
America without being troubled by its culture of material
excess. Indulged bodies, indulged children, and indulged
pets abound. This is not to say that there is no pain in
America, but until the terrible atrocities of Oklahoma City,
the World Trade Center, and the Pentagon, Americans had
known little approaching national suffering on their own
soil since their Civil War, nor any real insecurity since the
Great Depression. The consequence of this seems to be a

sense of entitled comfort and protection, as if suffering represents an unwarranted invasion of their rights.

I have remarked that America is the only country where more Christians go to church on Mother's Day than Good Friday and was once told that it is because Good Friday is "too depressing." The culture seems to encourage a sentimental faith that has difficulty with the central truth of the Gospel—that salvation can be wrought only by a suffering God, and that without the cross there can be no Easter.

Coming from South Africa, where so much suffering was the norm, this was the theme I often turned to when preaching in the United States.

—⚒—

There is power in faithful suffering! Where most religions offer escape from suffering and increases in comfort, the Christian faith makes this astounding claim. The Christian Bible speaks of *"going to Jerusalem, there to suffer much."* It speaks of *"taking up a cross,"* and of *"being given a share in Christ's suffering."*

This is hard to understand and even harder to live; but if you want to know whether God is alive, you must go, not to where all is well, but into places of brokenness and suffering.

This is what the disciples had to discover as they struggled to understand Jesus. At Caesarea Philippi Jesus asks his disciples about his identity, and Simon Peter finally answers, *"You are the Christ, the son of the living God."* Jesus says, "God has revealed that to you, Peter; . . . now let me give you the keys of the kingdom of Heaven." Then he tells them he must go to Jerusalem and suffer. Immediately Simon Peter recoils from this thought. *"This can't happen to you, Lord!"* Jesus has to rebuke him, because he still thinks as human beings think, not as God thinks. Then come the heavy words: *"If anyone wishes to be a follower of mine, he must leave self behind; he must take up his cross and come with me"* (Matthew 16:24).

It was much later that Peter understood all this more deeply. In his epistle he says, *"Dear friends, do not be bewildered by the fiery ordeal that is upon you, as though it were something extraordinary. It gives you a share in Christ's suffering, and that is cause for joy."*

If the cross means anything, it means we worship a suffering God. The most popular preachers of the day may promise something different—health, wealth, and heaven—but they mislead God's people. It is where the crosses of this world are planted that we will still find God.

There are depths of reality, dimensions of God, releases of healing energy, that flow into this world only through the power of faithful suffering.

When We Suffer *from* Something, God Is *with* Us

No amount of cushioning can protect us from the possibility of suffering. Illness and disease know no borders. Like the waters of the oceans that lap the shores of every continent, they come to touch even the most prosperous and affluent societies. In spite of our best efforts, the mortality rate of the human race is still a perfect 100 percent. We wrestle with a mystery, and our starting point must be to challenge the destructive myth that God can be the author of disease. *"It is not the will of the Father that any one of his little ones should suffer."* Those words of Jesus, and his whole ministry, convince me that God's declared will is to *"wipe every tear from [our] eyes"* and to put *"an end to death, and to mourning and crying and pain"* (Revelation 21:4).

I believe that day will come, but until then, suffering will be with us. When it comes, there is no way round it—only through it. And here is a deeper mystery: Evil though suffering is, contrary to God's will though it may be, those who suffer faithfully discover God in new and deeper ways and can become mediators of God to us.

My father died of heart disease in his late fifties. I was only twenty years old then, and as I watched his dramatic deterioration on my homecomings from university, I was angry. Why should this remarkable man be taken so soon? Why should I lose a father when I was just beginning to discover him as a friend? Then, when we were together for the last time, he said to me, "Peter, God has *trusted* me with this illness." Not, "God has *sent* this illness." He knew Jesus too well to waste time with a God who would ever *send* suffering. What he was saying was, "Now that I have this disease, God is trusting me with the bearing of it." And the way he bore it made a difference to others. Those who went into his room in his last weeks spoke of a sense of light in that place. Many told me they came out different.

As a young minister, my years in District Six—the ghetto where Cape Town's mostly poor, mixed-race people lived—shaped me profoundly. Among those I visited were a humble married couple who lived in two small rooms. The husband was a paraplegic, and each day someone would push his wheelchair the few blocks into the city where he would sell matches to make some money. His wife suffered from a twisted spine and hopped about with a crutch. They were always deeply grateful when I came to give them Holy Communion, and I went there more often than I needed to. I wish I could say it was because I cared so much for them, but the truth is more selfish: I went because I felt so close to God in that home. I discovered there why it is that when we want to be near God, *we reach out our hands for signs, not of success, but of suffering.* That is what the Bread and the Wine are about.

Don't ask me to explain it, but faithful suffering is never wasted. Somehow it allows this world to discover how closely God is with us.

When We Suffer Because of *Cruelty, Greed,* or *Neglect,* God Is *for* Us

Disease, of course, is not the major cause of human suffering. Neither is most suffering a mystery at all. It is caused by human cruelty, greed, and neglect.

At a meeting of the World Council of Churches in the 1980s I listened to the impassioned appeal of a medical missionary working in Central America. "The most widespread fatal disease in the world is not malaria or tuberculosis," he cried, "it is poverty!" He was right of course. When I worked in District Six, I conducted in those five years more child funerals than in all the other years of my ministry. I remember the anger I used to feel as I walked away from yet another tiny grave—the consequence of squalor, poor nutrition, and inadequate health care.

Poverty kills; and it is no accident that when God came among us in Jesus, he chose to be with, and *for*, the poor of the earth.

Next to that, the creator of the most widows and orphans, the purveyor of the most hideous suffering, is war. War, once the foolish, proud game of men on a battlefield, beating one another to pieces, now visits mainly innocent women, children, and elderly people. It is an interesting commentary on our denial of reality that we build memorials to the military personnel who die in our wars, but not to *the many more civilians whose deaths they bring about*. War can never be anything but evil. God will always be against the perpetrators of war, and *for* its victims.

Then there is oppression. In the twentieth century we came to recognize the reality of *institutional violence*—the violence caused, not so much by brutal blows and military weapons (although that is not excluded) but by the consistent violation of people's dignity through the denial of human rights.

Wherever people groan because of the suffering of poverty, war, and oppression, the Bible says that God is *for* them. The God of the Exodus "sees their misery, hears their outcry, takes heed of their sufferings," and will ultimately rescue them.

When We Suffer *for* Something, God Speaks *Through* Us

Sometimes we are called to suffer, not *from* something but *for* something, when suffering comes as a consequence of obedience, and when, because of our commitment to God's truth and justice, we must stand against the tide. Doing that always has consequences, but if that happens—and if we are faithful—God can speak words through us that can never be silenced.

Who can forget the powerful photograph that must have appeared in every newspaper in the free world in 1989? It showed a street in Beijing, empty except for a menacing column of tanks, and a young student, unarmed and alone, blocking their way with outstretched arms. We don't know his fate, but, knowing that regime, we can be sure that he suffered. We don't know his name, but nothing the Chinese government does can silence the ringing witness for freedom spoken by God through him that day.

If you look at the lives of the prophets, the strength of their witness lies not only in the weight of their words. It was their willingness to suffer for what they proclaimed that enabled God to speak so powerfully through them. And so it is with the prophets of our day.

On the wall of the grubby Memphis motel where Martin Luther King, Jr., was cut down by an assassin's bullet, there is a small memorial plaque, inscribed with these words from the old story of Joseph in Genesis:

> *"Here comes that dreamer. Now is our chance; let us kill him. . . .*
> *Then we shall see what will come of his dreams."*
> (Genesis 37:20)

The fullness of King's dream may not yet be realized, but his dying for that dream has guaranteed that it will continue to haunt the people of the United States year after year.

Never underestimate the words that God can speak through your life when you suffer for Godly truth, compassion, and justice. Through such lives, the word of God speaks.

When We Suffer *with* Others, God Is *in* Us

The deepest and most profound suffering comes, not as a chance blow, nor out of poverty or oppression, nor even as a consequence of obedience. It comes as a free choice, *when we choose freely to suffer with another, and the only thing that holds us is love.*

When it was becoming increasingly difficult to witness in South Africa, I visited West Berlin and met an amazing old man. His name was Bishop Scharf, a Lutheran bishop whose life had been literally laid alongside those who suffered. First, as a colleague of Dietrich Bonhoeffer, he had been imprisoned by the Nazis. Then, when the Soviets occupied East Germany, he championed those they persecuted and landed once more in a prison cell. Released finally to the West, Bishop Scharf again incurred the wrath of the state. He was concerned at what he heard about the way the infamous Baader-Meinhof terrorist gang were being treated by the West German authorities and began prison visits to them. The welfare of terrorists in prison was certainly not a fashionable or popular cause. This time, Bishop Scharf was not imprisoned, but he did suffer ostracism and rejection.

When we sat down together, I looked at this person who, for the sake of people he hardly knew, had lived a life of great hardship. I asked him for advice about offering a prophetic witness in times of deep injustice. He thought for a long moment, and then said that it was important for a Christian witness to be simple. "To be prophetic requires just four acts of solidarity with God's children. First, we must name the evil publicly and specifically. Second, we must pray for its victims by name. Third, we must go to those for whom we have prayed." "And what is the fourth?" I asked.

The old man's tone indicated he was simply stating the obvious: "*Suffer*," he said.

When we offer ourselves freely to suffer with the poorest, with the sufferers of this world, then God is in us. Certainly that is how Jesus understood the Spirit of God in his life. "*The Spirit of the Lord is upon me*," declared Jesus, "*because he has anointed me.*"

To do what?

> *To announce good news to the poor,*
> *to proclaim release for prisoners and recovery of sight for the*
>   *blind;*
> *to let the broken victims go free,*
> *to proclaim the year of the Lord's favor.* (Luke 4:18-19)

The story of Jesus is of one who suffered freely. He entered our condition, shared our humanity, embraced our pain, and experienced our grief. He died not only *for* us, but *with* us, hanging between two of our kind on Calvary. Only his love held him there. And because he chose to suffer, healing flowed for the world.

There are depths of reality,
    dimensions of God,
        and releases of healing energy,
            that flow into this world only through the power of
                faithful suffering.

It is so very difficult to understand why some suffering comes. It is painfully obvious why most suffering comes. But when suffering is borne faithfully, God can do deep and wonderful things. And when suffering is embraced by the Son of God himself, to be with and for us all—*that is the story of our salvation.*

11

These Wounded Hands Are God's!

Central Methodist Church, Johannesburg
Good Friday, 1980

Jesus said, "Reach your finger here; see my hands. . . ." Thomas
said, "My Lord and my God!" (John 20:27-28)

Lent was pilgrimage time at the Central Methodist Mission, with a meditation guide written by members of the congregation and a sermon series followed by lunch-hour and evening Holy Week services. On Holy Thursday, the Service of the Tenebrae was observed very publicly under a great wooden cross in the foyer, with doors open to the busy pedestrian mall outside. Then, in the darkness, some of us would carry that cross upstairs into the sanctuary, where it would tower over the worshipers who filled the church the next morning.

I have never been able to preach on Good Friday without being emotionally overwhelmed. Someone has said that the cross is for worship, not words, but we preachers have to stand up year by year in its shadow and try to pour the wonder of Calvary-love into the molds of ordinary speech, "to tell the old, old story of Jesus and his love."

I learned early that the task is impossible; yet each year, as if independent of our poor efforts, the message of the cross breaks out of those confines, takes life, and invades the hearts of the people with grace. Many of the most faithful members to join the CMM Church family traced their conversion to a Good Friday service of the cross.

—⚏—

When they reached the place called Golgotha and there they crucified him, I wonder, as the nails were positioned carefully in the center of his palms against the rough wood and the hammer poised, did the soldier pause?

"See my hands."

These hands of Jesus, about to be so cruelly violated with sharp iron, could tell so much about him. These hands were carpenter's hands, hands that had so often felt the texture of rough timber and shaped that timber expertly into something of beauty.

Carpenter's hands.

These hands were healer's hands, hands that had reached out with incredible sensitivity to touch the sore and broken places in people's bodies. These hands that had gently touched their wounds, bringing wholeness and help from pain. From these finger tips compassion flowed.

Healer's hands.

These were also powerful hands, hands that had knotted a whip out of cords and struck blows for truth, hands that had been lifted up against the spirits that shackled people's minds, casting those spirits out. These hands had been raised against wind and waves, bringing them into submission.

Powerful hands!

And these were praying hands, hands that had been lifted heavenward in supplication and in intercession for humankind, hands that had clasped each other in agonized wrestling with more than flesh and blood, which is what real prayer is about.

Praying hands.

I wonder, did they know what hands they were piercing? Did the soldiers pause?

The Bible says, "There they crucified him," and the nails were driven home. Carpenter's hands, now pinned to the roughest wood of all. Healer's hands, now themselves torn and bloody. Powerful hands now paralyzed. Praying hands wrenched apart. These wounded hands could tell so much, but all we hear are the hammer blows of Crucifixion.

The deepest secret of those hands was withheld that dark Friday. It was later, when the blood had dried and the corpse had been buried, when the sun had set and risen, and set and risen again, and when people were beginning to whisper of a miracle—it was then that their deepest secret was revealed. It was in the evening of the first day of the week, when one who doubted because he had seen what iron nails could do to quivering flesh, saw the familiar face and heard the loved voice: "Thomas, come and see, come and touch, come and feel these wounds."

And Thomas approaches. He reaches out, his hands touch the hands of Jesus, and he falls on his knees and cries, "My Lord and my God!"

These wounded hands are God's!

Today and every Good Friday, this is what we must know. You and I who so often speak and think of God as if of some distant managing director in the sky; you and I who in our pain cry out, "Where is God?" We must know that what was done on Golgatha was done to God. Didn't Jesus say to Philip, *"Anyone who has seen me has seen the Father?"* (John 14:9). If that is true, then Jesus could say, *"He who has pierced my hands has pierced my Father's heart."*

This means that what humanity did at Calvary was the ultimate wrong. It means that those nails poised in the soldier's hands become so many things:

• They become my cold pride and my sharpened hatred;

- They become my dark impulses of anger and selfishness,
- My lust for power,
- My lack of gentleness and care,
- My readiness to hurt and my refusal to love.

This is what those nails become. These are the barbs whose sharpened points are aimed through the hands of Jesus to the heart of God. And if this is true, then I see that sin is so much more than something I do wrong. Sin is a terrible torturing injury to God—because these wounded hands are God's.

God have mercy upon me. God was wounded for my transgressions. God was bruised for my iniquities.

—⚬—

But because these wounded hands were God's, *precisely because of that*, there is mercy.

It is William Manson who asks the question: "Where, where can such sin be undone? Not only forgiven but blotted out. Where? There is but one answer. It can be undone only in the heart of God. . . . Only the holy love of God can burn that sin to ashes so that it is no more."[1] Scripture tells us that God was in Christ—in Jesus—reconciling the world to Godself (2 Corinthians 5:19), and because of that, in all the horror of that Friday, God was there, and God was *doing something in the wounded body of Jesus*.

Jesus cries, "Father, forgive them!" and I hear the voice of the Father saying, "Yes, my son, that is what we are doing. I am here in what you are doing; I am here in what you are suffering; I am here in your forgiving."

The secret of these wounded hands is that on Calvary we see more than a man dying.

We see our God, reconciling the world, and you, and me, to Godself, reaching out through all our sin, reaching into all our lostness, reaching across all our failure and forgiving and healing and drawing us to Godself. It is our God who says, "Come, touch my hands, wounded and torn; and you will be whole."

Because these wounded hands were God's, this place, this Golgotha, this Calvary, this cross is the place we must go to worship God.

- We must know that at this place our sin is there doing the wounding, and we must repent with bitter tears.
- But we must also know that at this place God is there doing the forgiving, and we must receive that forgiveness with grateful wonder.

> O love of God! O sin of man!
>   In this dread act your strength is tried;
> And victory remains with love:
>   For He, our Lord, is crucified.[2]

These have always been the two mighty ingredients of new life—tears of repentance and the forgiveness of God. We know now, that because these wounded hands are God's, they are able to save. The Jesus who died for us comes to us on this Good Friday and says, "Come and feel these hands, these wounds and be not faithless, but believe." And you and I will fall on our knees and say with Thomas: *"These wounded hands are God's, they are God's! My Lord and my God!"*

Pray with me:

Lord Jesus Christ, thank you, thank you so very much for this day, for that place, for those hands, and for your Father's heart.

Help us each one to reach out to touch you, that by your wounds we may be healed.

Help us in response to your great, great love to say, "Jesus, I love you. I need you.

I repent before you. I confess that without you my life is empty."

Come, Lord Jesus, come into my life and work your healing and forgiving work there.

> O Master Carpenter of Nazareth,
> who at the last with wood and nails
>   purchased our whole salvation,
> wield well your tools in this your workshop,
> that we who come to your bench rough-hewn,
> may be fashioned to a truer beauty by your hand.[3] Amen.

---

1. William Manson, *The Way of the Cross* (London: Hodder and Stoughton, 1958), p. 87.

2. Frederick William Faber, "O come and mourn with me awhile," *The Methodist Hymn-Book* (London: Methodist Conference Office, 1933), no. 187.

3. Author Unknown. I found this "Carpenter's Prayer" in a newspaper cutting among my father's papers. It has always been precious to me.

Easter's Gift Of Peace

Central Methodist Church Chapel
Easter Evening, 1983

> *Late that Sunday evening, when the disciples were together*
> *behind locked doors, for fear of the Jews, Jesus came and stood*
> *among them. "Peace be with you!" he said, and then showed*
> *them his hands and his side. So when the disciples saw the Lord,*
> *they were filled with joy. Jesus repeated, "Peace be with you,"*
> *and said, "As the Father sent me, so I send you." And then he*
> *breathed on them, saying, "Receive the Holy Spirit! If you for-*
> *give anyone's sins, they stand forgiven; if you pronounce them*
> *unforgiven, unforgiven they remain." (John 20:19-23)*

Easter Morning at CMM was always a blaze of light and
joy. Tenebrae candles, extinguished in the darkness of
Maundy Thursday, now burned brightly again on each side
of the Christ candle. White and gold contrasted strongly
with the purple and black of Good Friday. A wonderfully
variegated congregation filled the sanctuary. The Risen
Christ was greeted with trumpet sounds and the full power
of the great organ.

On Easter evening, however, we met in the small chapel
near the street. Its muted wood paneling gave it a homely
feel; its worn carpet and somewhat battered pews spoke of

frequent use by passers-by. Worship here was intimate and less formal. The sermon often took the form of a Bible study.

Among our evening worshipers was a group of conscientious objectors, young men who were no longer comfortable in their home churches because of their refusal to serve in the *apartheid* regime's army. They were a reminder of the cost of the Gospel.

—m—

Fear Locks the Doors

It's fear, isn't it, that locks the doors! They were believers like us. The word of Resurrection had come to them, as it has come to us; but so had the darkness of night, and it's always harder to believe in the dark.

They were believers filled with fear, probably the most typical believers there are.

They were afraid of the very people Jesus told them never to fear—the people who could only destroy their bodies. But then, as now, the powers of this world's darkness seemed invincible. Had those powers not fashioned three crosses on a hill, and was there not plenty of timber for more?

Believers filled with fear.

If you were to ask me what has been the most paralyzing barrier to my ministry I would have to say it has been my fear—not a lack of gifts but a failure of courage. That's the place where my ministry has failed most often, just being scared.

I wonder whether that may not also be true for you? I think of some of the fears that bind God's people, some of the fears I have known.

- Fear of failure? Do you know the immobilizing anxiety born of the success syndrome that is so important to us?
- Fear of your past? Are there things about the past that you would pray most earnestly are never revealed?
- Fear of the future, of that uncertain tomorrow?
- Fear of dying? A very honest theologian once stood up in front of my Bible class and said, "I think I am a

Christian because I am afraid of dying." He was closer
to the truth than many of us would admit.
- Fear of living? If the statistics have anything to say, there
may be some people here tonight who have, at some
time, been afraid to go on living.
- Fear of the opinion of others and of the consequences of
being faithful? When the first of so many white people
angrily left this congregation because of our determination to integrate our membership, I remember how each
departure was like a blow in the solar plexus. I felt each
one go, and I'm sure that some of the pain was out of
sorrow for the loss of God's sheep; but I know that I was
also afraid of being known as the minister whose obsti-
nacy closed down South African Methodism's premier
pulpit.
- What about the very fear the disciples knew that night?
Fear of the Herods, the Pilates, the Caesars, the
Caiaphases—or the Verwoerds, the Vorsters, the Bothas[1]
who use the age-old fear of state repression? Has it
struck you that the government doesn't have to lock too
many of us up in its prisons. If it can frighten us suffi-
ciently, we will lock ourselves up just as those disciples
did and save the government the trouble.

Fear locks the doors and immobilizes us. Fear imprisons the
church in mediocrity and irrelevance. Fear forces us into quiet neu-
trality because that's the safest place for a fearful person and a fearful church.

The consequence is this—*About eighteen hours after the
Resurrection, the disciples of Jesus were still living as if he were dead!* If
we are a fearful Church and if we are fearful Christians, then we
will live as if Jesus is dead.

But thank God, there is good news. Thank God, *Jesus came and
stood among them.*

Jesus Meets Our Fears with His Shalom

Thank God that in spite of all the locks on all the doors, Jesus can
still get into the Church. He invades our places of fear and offers
the gift that only he can bring: *"Peace be with you!"*

95

Shalom was the daily Jewish greeting, but from the lips of Jesus it became something more. It was a tangible, transferrable gift that I want to give you from Jesus again.

What is this *shalom*?

Certainly it isn't going to be an absence of conflict. Outside of those locked doors there was a very rough world. Shalom is more like the place where an experienced sailor steers, the very eye of the storm. He knows that there will be found in the midst of the roaring wind a place of balance, a place where one force is countered against the other and held in a remarkable equilibrium. There, in the center of the storm—*shalom*.

How can we know this *shalom*?

Jesus gives his peace—and this is going to sound so simple—by *being there*. "*I will see you again*," he had said, "*and your hearts will rejoice, and no one will take your joy from you*" (John 16:22). Why? Because they would see him again! You remember when he came to their little boat, tossed about in the storm, how he trod the waves underfoot? You remember what he said to them? "Cheer up. Don't be afraid. It's me!" That doesn't sound like a profound theological statement. One would expect something a little more complex from the Son of God. But no, that's where *shalom* comes from:

"Don't be afraid, I'm here, I'm with you."

Admiral Richard Byrd, in his book entitled *Alone* tells the story of four months on the polar ice cap, absolutely alone in an underground hut, isolated, and thrown entirely upon his own resources. If those resources failed, only an act of rescue could save him. He tells how they did fail and describes how, having sent out a garbled distress signal, he dragged himself up the ladder day by day to the opening in the ice. There, utterly spent, he waited, listening. . . listening. . . always listening for a sound that might be different from the moaning of the wind. Finally, when all hope seemed lost, it came. He heard the clatter of a distant tractor clawing its way across the cruel ice toward him. It was not a sound we would associate with beautiful music, but Richard Byrd wrote that nothing in the world could sound so sweet. In that moment a deep sense of dependence overwhelmed him. He might have said, "Amazing Grace how sweet the sound."[2]

That is why we worship, why the first day of the week has always been the key to our faith. When we come in faith and cry:

"Jesus, stand among us in thy risen power," in that moment he comes. *He happens amongst us.* Worship is the opening of our hearts to the one who comes, and is. When he comes, he brings *"garlands instead of ashes, oil of gladness instead of mourner's tears, a garment of splendor for the heavy heart"* (Isaiah 61:3).

"So when the disciples saw the Lord, they were filled with joy" (John 20:20).

Oh, never, never lose that sense of simple dependence on the presence of Jesus in your life because sometimes it is all that you will have. He brings his *shalom* by standing among us as he stands among us now.

He Calls Us to Know Something of His Suffering

"Peace be with you," he said, and showed them his hands and his side. Here we have a mystery. The joy of recognizing him is bound up with the sight of his suffering. The gift of his peace is offered with wounded hands. Joy and peace and pain are strangely bound together. How can peace be married to pain? I don't know. What I do know is this: It is from those who have suffered that I have learned most profoundly about the *shalom* which passes all understanding.

Let me speak lovingly but plainly to those who present life in the Spirit as if it is a soft-drink commercial—full of fizz and froth and bubbles, all sugar and joy: *The Gospel record of Jesus imparting his Spirit is scarred by the remembrance of his pain.* The Church that would have it otherwise cannot have his Spirit, because it would fail to recognize him when he came. I do know that.

Let us be glad that living in the furnace of *apartheid* melts away cheap piety. What is left is something that you know is real, someone who you know is alive! And in the pain of witness in this land, we discover there is in that furnace with us another, whose "form is like unto a Son of God." Paul says if you have a part in Christ's suffering, you have a part in his consolation.

May I read these words to you? They are written by Winifred Holtby, and they scare me. She says this:

> I ask nothing better than to be allowed the very high privilege of writing with my heart's blood if that may be. I ask that I may suffer for those things that are brave and lovely and that I might be

permitted to love much. To serve to the uttermost of my capacity and to keep faith with that high vision which we call God. I shan't do it wholly, no one can do that. I only want never to stop caring. That's all. Other things don't matter.[3]

"Peace be with you!" he said, and then showed them his hands and his side.

He Sends Us with His Spirit to Intervene with His Pardon

Jesus repeated, "Peace be with you!" and said, "As the Father sent me, so I send you." Shalom is given not in withdrawal but in engagement. Other faiths may offer peace through retreat; Jesus says that his peace is given as we engage the world. We are sent as he was sent, into mission:

- Stable-born mission
- Controversial mission
- Healing mission
- Confronting mission
- Servant mission.

"That is how the Father sent me," he says, "Now I send you." And there is more. Listen to this:

> *Then he breathed on them, saying, "Receive the Holy Spirit! If you forgive any[one]'s sins, they stand forgiven; if you pronounce them unforgiven, unforgiven they remain"* (John 20:23).

These are difficult words. We who believe in the priesthood of all believers will reject interpretations implying that some priestly class can adjudicate the forgiveness, or otherwise, of people's sins. So what do these words mean?

Gordon Cosby, of the Church of the Savior in Washington, D.C., preached on this text.[4] This is the essence of his message:

> The Church has received power through the giving of God's Spirit, but the issue is not whether we have it, but rather if we use it. The Spirit is given us to declare God's

great act of forgiveness and reconciliation to the world, to announce God's intervention whereby he breaks the cycle of sin and death. If God had not intervened into history, into our individual lives, into specific situations, then we would have remained unhealed and unforgiven. Forgiveness is not a passive thing, it takes a mighty act of intervention.

Now, we are the body of Christ. We have received the Spirit of Christ, and we are called to intervene as God did in Christ, with the powerful word of pardon. Where we do that—where we declare sins forgiven—that pardon will be seen and experienced. Where we don't, it won't.

Do you get it?

If we are the *body* of Christ today, are we not called to intervene as God did in Christ? Are we not called to pronounce "the powerful word of pardon"? Are we not required to do so in our nation and our community? In every place where individual and corporate sin divides, oppresses, blinds and destroys people who God longs to set free? If we, as *body* of Christ, fail to do so, Christ has failed and this world will continue to be trapped, bound, and unaware that its liberator has come.

It's as simple as that—and as difficult. Where we do that, God's healing and pardon will be known. Where we don't, it won't.

Do you see it?

That seems to me to be the most powerful imperative for evangelism that I can find in Scripture. Somewhere, there are situations and people who only you can touch, places where only you can intervene to be the bearer of God's pardon.

You say, "Who, me? Really?"

Yes, you! I'm not necessarily talking about the big moments that make the headlines, where great statesmen reach out to each other across years of hatred and division—remember when Anwar Sadat first set foot on Israeli soil and held out his hand to Menachem Begin? Those are great moments of intervention in history and thank God for them—but I don't believe that that's where the action usually is. It is more likely to be at street level, in the hands of ordinary people like us.

In Moscow in 1941, the day came when the twenty thousand German army prisoners were to be marched through the streets in front of a population who had borne the burden of their cruelty. The pavements were crowded that day, mainly with women and children, those who had borne the brunt of the terrible suffering. Most of their menfolk were dead. Almost everyone had lost a husband, a son; and many had lost mothers, sisters, daughters because of this army, these people who were going to march down this street. You can imagine something of the atmosphere that day. At last they were going to see their hated enemy. There were angry mutterings and shouts of hate as the first of that defeated army, the Generals, prisoners yet still arrogant, strutted at the fore. People spat in the snow.

But then came the soldiers. And they were just boys really. Shuffling through the snow, their feet frostbitten, wrapped in newspapers. Many of them on makeshift crutches, others being led blind by one of their mates. And silence fell, and all you could hear was the shuffling of feet and the thumping of crutches. The shuffling of a defeated army of broken young boys.

Then there was a sudden movement. A woman, an old *babushka*, pushed herself through the crowd to the Russian soldiers guarding the pavement and said, "Let me through." Then this bent old woman rushed across to one of the gaunt German prisoners, and everybody held their breath. What was she going to do? Slap him? Spit on him?

She reached into her shawl and took out a crust of black bread, which she then pushed awkwardly into the pocket of a soldier, so exhausted that he was tottering on his feet. And all of a sudden from every direction, women began to hand over perhaps a cigarette, perhaps some bread, perhaps a piece of fish; and somehow the hatred was gone, enemies had ceased to be enemies. Why? Because one person, such an ordinary person, intervened into that cycle of hate and hurt and revenge with a simple act of pardoning love. That's all.[5]

"Well now," says Jesus, "my little band of frightened disciples, my beloved church, let my *shalom*, my presence, take away your fear; but let my peace hurt you just a little bit. Let it wound you so you know who I really am. And then as the Father sent me, unlock the doors and go!"

---

1. South African heads of state.

2. Richard Byrd, *Alone* (1938; reprint, Washington, D.C.: Island Press, 1984).

3. Winifred Holtby, British novelist, poet, journalist, and speaker from 1911-1935.

4. Gordon Cosby sent tapes of his sermons in the 1970s to CMM's Associate Minister, Reverend Trevor Hudson, to whom I owe this memory.

5. Yevgeny Yevtushenko, *A Precocious Autobiography*, trans. Andrew R. MacAndrew (New York: Dutton, 1963).

13

Strike a Blow
Against the Lie

Election Sermon,
Central Methodist Church
Johannesburg, May 3, 1987

Am I my brother's keeper? (Genesis 4:9)

Presented to the world as a bastion of Western values, South Africa's case unraveled mightily at election time when only the whites were permitted into the voting booths. As the struggle progressed, each whites-only election was accompanied by calls for concerned whites to boycott the polls and, in that way, to expose the charade. While the calls were persuasive, I found myself speaking against them. I continued to believe that because there were people willing to die for the vote, those with this privilege should use it, even within the limited parameters provided by South African "democracy." An additional reason was the valiant and important work of a few courageous opposition members of Parliament, who used parliamentary privilege

103

to expose atrocities and to come to the help of detainees and other victims.

Lest this position be misunderstood, election sermons needed to be very unambiguous. This was no time to mince words.

—⚉—

On Wednesday some two and a half million white South Africans will vote in an election that will decide the immediate future for thirty million of their fellows.

This is a painful time for a congregation such as ours. Most white South Africans do not have to look their voteless compatriots in the eye, but in this church we do. I would like those of us who have the vote, and those of us who do not, to take a moment to just look around and register one another's faces, remembering that God has made us one family.

Those whom God has joined in this place will be divided by the *apartheid* state on Wednesday.

In the sense that the election is already an act of gross injustice I understand anyone who says, "Because my brothers and sisters in Christ cannot vote, neither will I." That is one option.

I would urge another.

In preparing for today, I went back to John Wesley, who lived in a time when only a privileged aristocratic (and male) elite had the vote in a deeply divided England. His advice to those who had the franchise was "Each man must vote as if the whole moral outcome of the election depended on his one vote."

If you vote—and I would urge you to do so—what would Mr. Wesley's advice mean for this Wednesday? What thoughts should you carry into that voting booth?

If You Are a Christian, You Can't Leave *God* Out of the Voting Booth

When a person votes, even in our oppressive land, every effort is made to ensure confidentiality. This is right and proper, to protect each voter from intimidation. Nobody may help you, nor may anybody be near you. You make your cross on that ballot paper alone. . . .

Unless you are a Christian.

A Christian does nothing alone. If you are in Christ and Christ is in you, you can't leave God behind when you vote.

I will never understand the person who says, "My religion is one thing, my politics are something else." What does that person do on Election Day? Ask God to wait outside the voting booth?

Remember the words of the chorus "He Is Lord" so often sung:

> Ev'ry knee shall bow, ev'ry tongue confess, that Jesus Christ is Lord.

This Christ is hardly one to be told that he has nothing to do with my voting!

If Christ is Lord, nothing may operate outside of his reach. If I believe my Christian faith has nothing to say about my politics, I am saying God ought not to be God—and that is a nonsense. So if I have a vote and I am a Christian, I am responsible to God for how I exercise that vote, in the same way that I am responsible to God for every other decision I make.

I cannot leave God out of the voting booth.

If You Are a Christian, You Can't Leave Your *Neighbor* Out Either

One of the tough things about being a Christian is the call to love my neighbor as myself, but this is what I have to do. Jesus said that this commandment, together with loving God with heart and soul and mind and strength, is the greatest of them all. Ever since the story of Cain and Abel, we are bound to each other in an accountability that has deepened in the teaching of Jesus (Genesis 4:8-10). Cain denies being his brother's keeper; Jesus commands us to be our brother's *brother* and our sister's *sister*. He calls us to be neighbor to all.

Therefore, voting with a Christian conscience means voting so that my neighbor will enjoy all that I want to enjoy. It can never mean less than that; and if this is true for any Christian anywhere, how much more true for us in this election! I say this because *every one person who is privileged to vote in South Africa has five neighbors who are not*. If you are voting, imagine those five people looking over your shoulder when you make your cross.

There is something very fundamental here: I know of no place where the difference in being a Christian is so marked as in the world of politics.

- So often politicians seek to make their policies attractive; Christians must seek policies that are right.
- Politicians tailor their policies to the selfishness of the hearer; Christians are commanded to seek their neighbor's welfare.
- Politicians whip up our dark prejudices and fears; Christians are called to rise above them with the love that includes all and casts out fear.

A Christian voter will be different! A Christian voter in South Africa will want to meet the eyes of those who have no vote and not have to look away in shame. The world says, "Vote for yourself and your children—the only ones who matter." Christ calls us to make another choice: In the Garden of Gethsemane, Jesus prays for the world and says, "Father, for their sakes I sanctify myself."

So when you go into the voting booth, you will have company:

- The migrant worker whose family is not allowed to live with him;[1]
- The person in a Hillbrow flat, waiting for the Group Areas Inspector to throw him and his family out;[2]
- The detainee who is being tortured for doing nothing more than demonstrate for the right to this vote;
- The mother trying to bring up her children in one of *apartheid*'s hostile dumping grounds;[3]
- The child caught up in township violence, grown old and hard while still a teenager.

These five people will be with you—and countless others.

If You Are a Christian, You Can't Leave the *Truth* Out of That Voting Booth Either

Election time in South Africa is a time for lies when, more than any other, it should be the time for truth.

This election is more informed by lies than any I remember because there are so many more laws to stop us knowing the truth. The state of emergency has put us at the mercy of a government-controlled radio and television service, and a government-controlled Bureau of Information.

How do we get at the truth? Listen to these words of Jesus: *"If you dwell (take up residence) within the revelation I have brought . . . you shall know the truth, and the truth will set you free"* (John 8:31-32).

The Christian will measure events and opinions against the revelation of Jesus—the Word of God. When you live in the Word of God, you can see things more clearly. Jesus told his disciples that the Holy Spirit would help them discern the truth. The Spirit, he said, *"will confute the world, and show where wrong and right and judgement lie"* (John 16:8-9). For thirty-nine[4] years now the Church in this land has weighed this government's policies against the Word of God. Over all of these years, with growing certainty we have had to say:

- Your policies are evil.
- They are based, not on the truth but on an enormous lie.
- This lie has led our land to the edge of civil war.

The lie, of course, says that the differences between people are more important than the things we have in common, and that our racial and cultural identity is more important than our common humanity.

That is the lie that has led us to disaster. It is the lie of *apartheid*. Be sure that the state of emergency is not there to keep you safe—it is there to protect the lie.

Today, the church of Christ in this land stands up and says: "A vote for *apartheid* is a vote for a lie. A vote for the Group Areas Act is a vote for a lie. A vote for anything that classifies people by race is a vote for a lie."

God is going to destroy this lie. Be absolutely assured of that.

The choice is simply whether we will allow change to come in God's way, or whether God will have to use the world's way; but one way or the other, God will destroy this lie.

God does not want to destroy it through bloodshed and violent conflict, but through the way of the cross, through a mighty change of heart amongst God's people; and the first people who must change are those who have believed the lie, supported the lie, voted for this lie.

When we light our candle of Peace and Justice[5] every Sunday, we pray for those who are oppressed, that they may be set free. That prayer will only come true—can only come true—if those who pray it will risk obeying God.

If you are one of those privileged minority who will vote on Wednesday,

- Don't leave God outside;
- Don't leave your neighbor outside;
- Don't leave the truth outside.

Take all of them into that voting booth and strike a blow against the lie.

---

1. Migrant laborers were recruited for work in the mines and other industries from far-flung rural areas. They were housed in single-sex hostels in the cities, and lived there for at least nine months of the year. Their families were not permitted to join them.

2. The Group Areas Act determined residential areas on a strictly racial basis. Hillbrow is Johannesburg's flatland, filled with high apartment blocks, and was reserved for white occupants only. By 1987, however, thousands of illegal black residents were filling empty apartments.

3. Three and a half million black South Africans were forcibly moved from their ancestral homes to so-called Bantu Homelands, usually in very inhospitable rural areas.

4. Referring to the time elapsed since whites elected the *apartheid* government.

5. The Candle of Peace and Justice was modeled on the symbol of Amnesty International, surrounded by a coil of barbed wire, first introduced in South Africa on the altar of the Central Methodist Mission in Johannesburg, and gradually used more widely in congregations committed to the struggle against *apartheid*. In the liturgy a place was made for the lighting of this candle after remembering those suffering the latest acts of oppression, then joining in the prayer for Africa.

14

God Has No Favorites

National Radio Broadcast,
Central Methodist Church
June 5, 1988

When he comes, he will confute the world, and show where
wrong and right and judgement lie. (John 16:8)

I now see how true it is that God has no favorites. (Acts 10:34)

To continue using the national broadcasting medium, there was the need to use code words, understood by the suffering majority in our land, yet remaining just inside the bounds of what one guessed the authorities would tolerate. They did not appreciate this approach, however, and tensions with the South African Broadcasting Corporation were reaching a breaking point.

Their demand for sermon texts in advance had to be refused. (Being a notoriously last-minute sermon writer, I could honestly claim that God never spoke to me early enough.)

It was clear that CMM's days on radio were now numbered. I decided to offer a simple Bible study on racism, but it didn't make the air in its entirety, because, in the middle of this sermon, the little red light in the pulpit was extinguished; we were cut off the air.

It was the beginning of the end. The South African Broadcasting Corporation claimed it had been a technical fault, but after our next broadcast in Advent, entitled "The Dangerous Baby of Bethlehem," we were taken off the air permanently. This time the offense was our lighting of the Candle of Peace and Justice and our prayers for the victims of *apartheid*.

After a hiatus of two years, following the release of Nelson Mandela from prison, the South African Broadcasting Corporation found it politic to invite CMM back on the air. I enjoyed opening that service with the words, "As I was saying when we were so rudely interrupted . . . "

—⁂—

In the first fifteen chapters of the book of Acts there are a number of themes. The birth and spread of the early Church are there. The apostles' determination to obey God rather than human authority is recounted, together with their first experiences of persecution. We also find the dramatic martyrdom of Stephen and the conversion of Saul the Pharisee to Paul the Apostle.

But there is another theme: Throughout these fifteen chapters we see the Holy Spirit coaxing, challenging, and convicting the first Christians about a deeply wrong attitude and a dangerous sin.

Put quite simply, the early Christians practiced *spiritual apartheid*. They thought the Gospel and the gift of the Holy Spirit were for Jews only. Because of their upbringing as a separated, exclusive people, they never questioned this assumption. When they became Christians, and even after they received the Holy Spirit at Pentecost, this exclusivism remained deeply ingrained within them.

Gentiles were different. Gentiles were inferior. God's gifts could not be for them.

That's why one of the first tasks of the Holy Spirit was to confute this attitude and prove them wrong. The remarkable step-by-step strategy the Spirit used to introduce the apostles to the rest of the human race makes fascinating reading.

First, some Samaritans, people who had been segregated from the Jews for eight hundred years, are converted through Philip. God seems to want them in the church too! (Acts 8:4-13).

Then this same Philip meets an African from Ethiopia, hitches a ride with him, and before long they stop for this person to be baptized—a black man in the Church! (Acts 8:26-40).

Not long after that, Peter, the leader of the Church, has a strange dream and receives an invitation from Cornelius the Roman—not just a Gentile, but an enemy. When he gets to the home of Cornelius, he discovers and confesses his prejudice, and declares a new conviction about it:

I need not tell you that a Jew is forbidden by his religion to visit or associate with a man of another race; yet God has shown me clearly that I must not call any man profane or unclean.
(Acts 10:28)

Peter is saying, "This goes against everything I have been brought up to believe, but because God told me to come, I'm here."

A little while later, when he hears Cornelius' testimony of simple faith, Peter recognizes the power of God in his life and cries, *"I now see how true it is that God has no favorites!"* (Acts 10:34).

Unfortunately, prejudice and old attitudes of exclusion don't easily lie down and die. When Peter gets back to Jerusalem, he is faced by a bitter attack from others in the Church. *"You have been visiting men who are uncircumcised,"* they said, *"and sitting at table with them!"* (Acts 11:3). This is too much for their sensibilities. But Peter recounts the Cornelius story with such power that their objections are temporarily silenced.

Up to now God's Spirit has dealt gently with these prejudiced Christians. They have had to swallow hard and accept Samaritans; but there is some comfort in the fact that Samaritans are, after all, half Jewish. Perhaps the Ethiopian and Cornelius the Roman could be included too, because they were "God-fearers"—students, at least, of the Jewish faith.

But now comes the bombshell. At Antioch, some anonymous Christians begin preaching to the Gentiles—people with no Jewish religious links whatsoever—and "a great many became believers and turned to the Lord." God must have a sense of humor because

Barnabas rushes from Jerusalem to Antioch and is convinced by what he sees. He goes straight to Tarsus to invite Saul, the ex-Pharisee, to become the minister of this first all-Gentile congregation! For a year, Barnabas and Saul, who has become Paul, work as ministers to the Gentiles; and it is here, at Antioch where barriers of prejudice are broken, that the followers of Jesus are first called "Christians" (Acts 11:19-26).

This is not the end of the problem, however. The forces of conservatism and prejudice begin to mobilize in Judea (Acts 15:1). They want a showdown. They want a "Jews only" Church, and if they can't have that, the only concession they'll make is to grudgingly accept Gentiles only after they have first become circumcised Jews. The lines are now drawn, and the only way to deal with this grievous controversy is to call all the Christian leadership together in Jerusalem. The first ever Church conference takes place. *It is here, at the Council of Jerusalem, that the Holy Spirit does battle with prejudice in the Church.*

Barnabas and Paul testify to God's mighty acts among the Gentiles, and Peter helps swing things with his newly enlightened views and a powerful declaration about the Gentiles: *"We believe it is by the grace of the Lord Jesus that we are saved, and so are they"* (Acts 15:11).

At the end of that council, the first official decision of the Church is agreed, setting its face firmly against prejudice and welcoming all into its fellowship. This is the last time Jews and Gentiles in the Church are referred to as "We" and "They."

The Spirit Is Wrestling with God's Church Here and Now

I've repeated this story because many of us in South Africa need to discover that God has no favorites. Too many of us think we can be exclusive and Christian at the same time. Just as the Holy Spirit had to wrestle with the early Christians and confute them—prove them wrong—so the Holy Spirit of God is wrestling with stubborn prejudice among people who claim to be Christians here. God is hurt and angered by the resurgence of naked racism and bitter prejudice that we see around us. When people in our land use the name of Jesus to justify discrimination against their fellows, that is the final insult to God.

Of course it's hard to change. Peter found it hard, Saul the Pharisee found it hard, but they were followers of Jesus and his Holy Spirit had to be obeyed. Listen again to Jesus. He promises that when the Holy Spirit comes,

> *He will confute the world, and show where wrong and right and judgement lie. He will convict them of wrong, by their refusal to believe in me* (John 16:8-9).

Those who hold on to prejudice in defiance of the Holy Spirit are actually refusing to believe in Jesus. The first fifteen chapters of the book of Acts tell us so.

What then shall we do?

How does someone with deeply rooted, poisoned attitudes, change? How is the Holy Spirit to win God's battle in South Africa?

Let me give three thoughts that may help us.

- **People change when they discover that their lives are enriched by the very people they despised.** That's what happened to Peter, and Saul and Barnabas as well. Cornelius enriched Peter's life. Ministry among Gentile people in Antioch convinced Saul and Barnabas that their past prejudices were absurd, stupid, and wrong.

  When we make real contact with the people we exclude, God shows us how impoverished our lives have been without them.
- **People change when the Church listens to God and obeys.** At the Council of Jerusalem, those present were listening for God. They ultimately placed God's word above their own pride and prejudice, and came to the painful conclusion that they had been wrong.

  When the Church of Jesus Christ in our land is radically obedient to the Christ who says we are all one, when people see the Church living the unity we preach, committed to justice and inclusion for all—then change will come.

- **People change when we really trust our fears to Jesus.**
  So much of our prejudice is rooted in fear and insecurity.
  Really believing in Jesus means letting go of those fears.
  It means learning to trust much more deeply than we
  have ever before. We sometimes sing,

Make me a captive, Lord, and then I shall be free. Force me to
render up my sword, and I shall conqueror be.[1]

Only those who have learned that the letting go of self
opens our lives to the love of Christ, are able to see that
the letting go of prejudice, pride, and privilege opens
God's way for a new land of peace and justice.

The problems of our land are not just political problems. At their
deepest level they are profoundly spiritual. We need to heed the
Holy Spirit, who has confuted our behavior and shown us that our
ways are wrong. There is no question about that. The judgment of
God is upon this land and upon us.

But God's Spirit will not abandon us. The Spirit comes to lead us
into all truth. The question now is whether, like those first
Christians, we are willing to trust the truth of Christ enough to let
our old ways go, and discover with joy that God has no favorites.

---

1. George Matheson, "Make Me a Captive, Lord," *The United Methodist Hymnal* (Nashville: The United Methodist Publishing House, 1989), no. 421.

15

Sentence Them to Church!

On the Desecration of Central Methodist Church
Sunday, June 19, 1988

O God, the heathen have set foot in thy domain
defiled thy holy temple. (Psalm 79:1)

They will do these things because they do not know either the
Father or me. (John 16:3)

Let us then go to him outside the camp, bearing the stigma that
he bore. (Hebrews 13:13)

Wednesday night, June 15, 1988, was the eve of our twelfth remembrances of the Soweto shootings, and for the occasion our Sunday school children had decorated CMM's foyer with many moving prayers for peace.

That night the exterior walls received a different decoration. They were defaced with crude political graffiti, purporting to have been smeared there by some of the human rights organizations to whom we had given sanctuary. One of CMM's janitorial staff saw the perpetrators at work in the dark hours. The next day, when security police surrounded the church building to monitor our June 16 services, he saw one of them again—now amongst them. The security police had been responsible for defacing God's house.

—⁂—

As you arrived for worship today, I wonder if you felt as I did on Thursday morning. First shock and disbelief, and then a deep pain to see this place which we love and cherish, this lovely house of God, daubed and violated and made ugly in the darkness of night by nameless, hate-filled people.

Yesterday one of our members saw it for the first time "Don't speak to me," she said, "or I'll burst into tears."

In this coming week we hope to remove the outward signs of this blasphemy, but the hurt of it will be with us for a long time. With the psalmist we cry, "O God, the heathen have set foot in your domain and defiled your holy temple." What makes it worse is that this was no act of sudden passion. If the walls of Central Church had been daubed with swastikas and racist symbols, that would have been no less a desecration, but it would have been more easily understood.

What happened on Thursday morning was a premeditated act, planned coldly and deliberately by the system, not only to insult this Church but to discredit some of the organizations we have sheltered and accommodated in their work for peaceful change and greater justice in South Africa. This was done to make it look as if some of these organizations would defile a house of God, and because most people who pass by do not think very deeply, many have possibly been deceived into thinking just that. On Thursday morning one old gentleman said as much. As he stood looking at those crude slogans, he said. "That's how they pay you back for feeding them downstairs in the People Center."[1] Now, we all know who he meant by "they" and "them."

The perpetrators of this desecration were not South Africa's ordinary brand of racist fanatics taking out their hate on our walls. Jesus warned that some people would act against the Church out of a sense of duty. I believe that when we unmask them, we will find they were doing their duty. This act is part of a wider campaign to bring the Church into disrepute, to undermine respect for the moral authority and the witness of Christians in our land today.

How must we respond to the working of this evil? Jesus says that before we come to the altar with any gift for God, if we have anything against our neighbor, we should first put it right.

I have much against that neighbor right now, so I shall try to do so.

We Still Have to Hate the Sin, But Not the Sinner

No matter how angry we feel, Christians are not permitted to have enemies. Jesus outlawed the concept of "enemy." By his attitude to those who opposed him, he made the enemy obsolete.

Paul the apostle made it clear that to locate your foe in the person of a fellow human being is a mistake:

> *Our fight is not against human foes, but against cosmic powers, against the authorities and potentates of this dark world, against the superhuman forces of evil in the heavens.* (Ephesians 6:12)

When I first saw the violence done to this house of God, I had an overwhelming longing to see the faces of those who had done it and to lash out at them; but that first, instinctive reaction was a mistake. It is like blaming the boil for the poison in the blood stream.

Far more dangerous and evil than the people who did this are the forces that drive them: hatred, prejudice, ideological imprisonment, fear, untruth—these are the real enemies of us all. These are the superhuman forces against which we wrestle, and they have taken up residence in the minds of too many South Africans.

Let us not have our minds so diverted by anger at the persons who did this. They are not so much enemies as victims. The real enemy is what drives them.

A Challenge to the Church's Task

When Jesus warned that the world would hate his followers, he said people would act against the Church because "they do not know either the Father or me."

Can you imagine anyone who really knows and loves God going around in the dead of night desecrating houses of worship? Of course not! So it means that those who did this simply don't know God. That means they are the people the psalmist talks about: "O God, the heathen have defiled your holy temple!"

Oh, they may have some god. Most people do. My guess is that theirs is the tribal god of the white race, of their language and narrow nationalism. They bow to the idols that so many worship in this land, *but they do not know the God and Father of our Lord Jesus Christ.*

That's why, if we identify them, we will prosecute them, and when they are found guilty, I shall ask the magistrate to sentence them to worship here every Sunday for six months.

- To sing with us,
- To pray with us,
- To pass the peace of Christ with us,
- To hear the liberating Good News of God's grace with us,
- To break bread with us,

So they may find God!

Let this be a reminder that our task, begun in this city a century ago, is unfinished. While there are still people with this kind of darkness in their souls, we have a job to do! Our task is to preach and practice the Gospel of love and justice, reconciliation and peace, and so to demonstrate it that lives such as these are released from their prisons of hate.

On our altar the Candle of Peace and Justice reminds us that "it is better to light a candle than to curse the darkness." Let's remember that today.

A Reminder of Who the Church Really Is

> We love the place, O God,
> wherein thine honor dwells.[2]

Of course we do! We have a deep attachment to this sanctuary because this is where deep things have happened in our souls. These walls are soaked with the memories of God's touch upon our lives.

But . . . bricks and mortar do not make the Church.

In 1985 Elizabeth and I traveled to the northern border of war-torn Namibia.[3] A courageous Methodist pastor, Ludwig Hausiko, himself a refugee, risked land mines to drive us into the bush on the banks of the Kunene River. I was going to preach to our people.

Leaving his pickup truck, we followed Ludwig along a narrow path in the high grass until we entered a small clearing. Here, in this perfectly swept space, logs had been placed at careful intervals, an "aisle" had been carefully swept in the dust between them. Up front, under a spreading thorn tree, mounted on four tree branches planted in the earth was a flattened paraffin tin. This was to be my "pulpit." All so very different from this great sanctuary here in Johannesburg!

Then the people came.

They came through the bush with the tread of those who had learned to walk warily. They were women, all of them. There were no men. The war had taken the men. These women and young girls all wore the same garments—a potato or flour sack with holes cut for head and arms. Survival in the midst of a bush war had long since relegated pretty dresses to a very low priority. At first sight, a straggling group of pathetic refugees.

But not so!

You see, they were singing as they came, and each one had in her hand a tree frond, and they waved these fronds gracefully in the air as they sang the praises of God with joy on their faces. As we listened, I remembered the joyful songs of broken and downtrodden people on a long ago hillside when palms were lifted in salute to a young prophet on his way to Jerusalem:

"Hosanna! Blessed is he who comes in the name of the Lord! Hosanna!" (from Luke 19:38)

We had Church that day! That little clearing in the war-ravaged bush on the Angola border became a soaring cathedral whose roof was blue sky with walls of elephant grass, and whose songs flew direct to the heart of God.

Being the Church of Jesus is ultimately not about this place. We all surely know that. While we cherish and reverence its walls, they are simply a temporary enclosure for things bigger and wider and deeper.

When this place is scarred and violated by hate, we need to remember that being the Church of God means being scarred much more deeply than that.

In the book of Hebrews, we are reminded that Jesus suffered "outside the gate"; and if we are to find him, we need to "go outside the camp, bearing the stigma that he bore."

Scripture goes on to say:

> *For here we have no permanent home, but we are seekers after a city which is to come. Through Jesus, then, let us continually offer up to God the sacrifice of praise, that is, the tribute of lips which acknowledge his name, and never forget to show kindness and to share what you have with others; for such are the sacrifices which God approves.* (Hebrews 13:12-16)

Being the church of Jesus means living like that, and it also means learning to bear the stigma he bore. The marks of his suffering are to be carried, not merely on these walls, but in our hearts.

---

1. The People Center was Johannesburg's first integrated restaurant, opened as an act of witness against the laws requiring segregated amenities. It was operated by CMM for fourteen years.

2. William Bullock, "We love the place, O God," 1854.

3. At this time the war to free Namibia from South African control was raging and the South African military had more or less free rein over northern Namibia and southern Angola. As president of the Methodist Church, I was visiting our work among Angolan refugees hiding in the bush.

16

I Am So Sorry, Mama

Funeral of Stompie Sepei at Tumahole Township
February 25, 1989

A little child shall lead them. (Isaiah 11:6)

But if a man is a cause of stumbling to one of these little ones who have faith in me, it would be better for him to have a millstone hung around his neck and be drowned in the depths of the sea. Alas for the world that such causes of stumbling arise! (Matthew 18:6-7)

The murder of fourteen-year-old Stompie Sepei was a disgraceful chapter in the liberation struggle. He was the youngest of around fifteen traumatized youths given sanctuary in a Methodist manse in Soweto. Stompie, together with four older youths, was abducted by thugs linked to Mrs. Winnie Mandela, imprisoned in her home nearby, and falsely accused of improper sexual behavior with the Methodist minister[1] who cared for them. They were brutally whipped and beaten. One youth escaped and reached my office at Central Methodist Mission with the news. We heard that Stompie had also been accused of being an informer, had suffered the worst beating of all, and had not been seen again.

This is not the place to detail the agonizing hostage drama that ensued. The following days were an ethical, political, and legal nightmare, some of the most painful of my Episcopal leadership. At the center of it all was the spouse of the most famous political prisoner in the world. Winnie Mandela had become an international icon of the struggle. The police were not an option because they were the enemies of the people and had harassed Winnie for years for political reasons; so it was up to the Church, in collaboration with the underground leadership in Soweto, to pry the youths from Mrs. Mandela's house. After protracted negotiations, two of them were finally released into my care, traumatized but alive. They were adamant that Winnie was present and participated in the assaults in her home. The third survivor chose a different sanctuary.

Stompie never came out. We later learned that the same night he was kidnapped, he was taken from the house, his throat was slit, and he was left in the *veld* to die. When his body was found, his funeral was attended by thousands. It was an emotional outburst of anger and fear.

Mrs. Mandela was much later found guilty of kidnapping, but the judge accepted testimony providing an alibi for the actual beatings. Some of those who provided that testimony have since recanted before the Truth and Reconciliation Commission.

As we wrestled with this crisis, I had a close-up view of the struggle within underground liberation movement circles. Some to whom I pay tribute in this sermon believed it crucial to sever ties with Mrs. Mandela, no matter what the cost. Those in exile, more concerned with the political fallout, fudged. In the short term, she was disciplined; but later, under pressure from the exiles, she was brought back into the fold and continued to embarrass South Africa's new government. More importantly, failure by the African National Congress to deal firmly with this criminal disaster within its own ranks, seriously compromised its moral authority on issues of criminal impunity as the new nation was born.

—ɯ—

There are moments in our history when all the tangled pain and violence and division and horror of our bleeding land seem to coalesce and confront us all. This is such a moment.

As I stand here, I feel the burden of all the years . . .
    of all the suffering
        by so many people
            in so many ways.

It's all here today, represented by this broken little body and this mother in mourning.

This funeral is a parable of South Africa's pain.

I Speak to You, Mrs. Sepei

I am sorry, Mama.

I am sorry that I had to come into your home and tell you that your child,
    blood of your blood,
        flesh of your flesh,
            bone of your bone . . . was in all likelihood dead.

I watched your face . . . and in that face I saw the faces of too many mothers of South Africa. I saw the disbelief, the hope that refused to die, and in my heart I knew that your hope was doomed.

I said a prayer with you and we wept together.

And then I left.

Today you have the proud sorrow of a great funeral. You join that long line of grieving mothers who have buried their children amongst vast throngs singing of freedom.

But tomorrow you will be alone. And your son will still be dead.

I am so sorry, Mama.

I Speak to You, Stompie

I did not know you well. You once sat in my office after a protest service at the Central Methodist Mission. There had been a march from *Khotso* House to the church. I thought you were lost—waiting for an elder brother perhaps?

Then I was told that you were waiting for the security police to get tired of waiting downstairs so you could escape.

I was told that you had led the march!

And I looked at you, and in my mind I cried, "Dear God! What have we done?" That a mere child, who should be playing marbles in a backyard somewhere, or running with your friends in the *veld*, or chattering in a school room, is robbed of his childhood and has the tired look of an old man already in his eyes.

And I thought of the words of Jesus: *"Let the little ones come to me"* and:

> *if anyone puts a stumbling block in the way of any of these little ones, it would be better for him if a great millstone were hung around his neck, and he were thrown in the depths of the sea.* (from Mark 10:14, Matthew 18:6)

Your terrible and violent death was an unspeakable crime; and when I think of the way you died, I am deeply angry. But before your body was so brutally broken, your childhood was already dead. *South Africa killed your innocence long ago.* That is the greater infamy and deserves the deeper anger.

You loved coming to Church. In another land you might have been a choirboy, but South Africa made you a boy general. God forgive us. I am not proud of that.

I am so sorry, Stompie.

Rest in peace. You found little in your short life.

I Speak Now to Those Gathered Here

Bow your heads for this child. Salute his courage. *But do not injure him any further by using this funeral as a platform for revenge.* If there are those who have come to stoke the fires of retaliation, you should go home, because you do him no honor.

As the facts of his dying have emerged, these past weeks will be remembered as weeks of shame and of profound tragedy. These weeks have probed beneath the surface of South Africa's pain and exposed the deeper, hidden wounds these hateful years have carved into an oppressed people's soul:

- the erosion of conscience,
- the devaluing of human life,
- the reckless resort to violence,
- the evasion of truth.

There is a choice to be made today about these wounds. Either we will open them wider, or we will seek—for Stompie's sake, and hundreds more like him—to heal them.

I am told that he could recite the Freedom Charter[2] by heart. However deep our outrage at the thought of his last hours, this moment is a test of how seriously the people take the spirit of that charter, which outlaws the dark desire for vengeance and speaks of "fighting side by side," not destroying one another.

If anything can be learned at this place, it is surely how destructively lies can divide the people. How, in a land where law has been used to hurt, lawlessness can become a virtue. How, in a society of violent oppression, the oppressed can be turned to violent division.

This is not a time for the rhetoric of hate. Slogans can turn people to killing, but slogans cannot raise the dead. Retaliation will not bring this child to life; all it will do is gather another crowd, at another place, for another funeral.

I have spoken of the wounds *apartheid* has made in our souls. But the struggle has also brought forth strength. If anything good can be said to have come out of this tragic death, it has been the moral strength of those young leaders of a wounded people, who, in spite of all they have suffered, still know right from wrong, can still discern the difference between justice and revenge, and will risk political loss rather than compromise the integrity of the struggle.

I salute those who believe that in the new South Africa we are struggling for, a mourning mother's pain and the life of a *Tumahole* child are infinitely more important than the loss of political face.[3]

I Speak to the Oppressive Rulers of This Nation

Yes, this tragedy casts an ugly stain on the struggle for freedom; but before you are tempted to take comfort in it, remember this: Long before his life was so brutally taken, Stompie Sepei was already willing to lay it down. And there are millions like him. If a fourteen-year-old child will die for freedom, nothing can stop freedom coming.

So, from this place of death and burial, hear the message: You will not kill the idea of liberty and you cannot bury the vision of a new South Africa. Let those still holding on to power know this.

And when that freedom day comes, we will remember the Stompies and know they have had a part in fulfilling the scriptures that declare: *"a little child shall lead them"* (Isaiah 11:6).

---

1. The Reverend Paul Verryn was later fully exonerated of this damaging charge at the Truth and Reconciliation Commission hearings. He went on to succeed me as Bishop ot the Central District of the Methodist Church of Southern Africa.

2. The Freedom Charter was the basic declaration of principles of the African National Congress. It was adopted and signed at the Congress of the People in 1955.

3. This refers to those few political leaders, like Murphy Morobe and Azar Cachalia, who had the courage to publicly denounce Mrs. Mandela's actions in spite of powerful attempts to avoid holding her accountable.

17

When God Turns the Tide

Sunday after President De Klerk announces
an end to apartheid
February 11, 1990

We must obey God rather than men. (Acts 5:30)

If this idea . . . is of human origin, it will collapse; but if it is from God, you will never be able to put them down, and you risk finding yourself at war with God. (Acts 5:37-38)

On February 2, 1990, a few months after Mr. F. W. de Klerk succeeded P. W. Botha as state president, he used the opening of Parliament to announce a complete reversal of policy, signaling the end of forty-two years of *apartheid*.

It was an electrifying moment across the land. Those of us who had tested his strength leading the great November 1989 marches of the thirty thousand in Cape Town, and the twenty-five thousand in Johannesburg had been surprised by the unusual absence of armed police and soldiers. There was promise of a more flexible regime. But few could have expected the totality of this capitulation. The liberation movements were to be unbanned, Nelson Mandela was to be freed within days, exiles were to be invited home, and negotiations for a new South Africa were to begin.

This sermon attempted to interpret this climactic moment in the light of Scripture. Preached at CMM just

nine days after De Klerk's speech, it was also offered in
June that year in Duke University Chapel in the United
States. Because it included a little more of what happened
around the world in 1989–90, I have added portions of that
version.

—⁓—

You and I are privileged to be living through one of the semi-
nal moments of God's providence. There are moments in history
when a new mood grasps a whole nation, pushing fear and hate
back into the shadows where they belong and setting us free to
hope again.
Such a moment is now.
Who would have dreamed? Who could have believed that such
a moment would come? When hope reborn could rise so powerfully among us! When prayers prayed so long around this candle
could be so decisively answered.

- Around the world we have seen Berlin's wall crumble—
  and with it the temples of Marxism's false god.
- In spite of South Africa's military might, we have witnessed independence come to Namibia, ending its long
  night of oppression.
- We have watched with the world as Nelson Mandela
  walked out of those prison gates to freedom.

It is as if God, grown suddenly impatient with our whoring after
the false gods of totalitarianism, colonialism, and racial oppression,
has dealt history a sudden blow to set whole segments of humanity off on a new course—away from madness.
So, in South Africa, the tide now flows irresistibly toward justice.
Eddies there are sure to be, with sometimes a contrary wind whip-
ping the surface, but beneath that surface the flow is strong and
sure. "When these things begin to happen," said Jesus, "stand
upright and hold your heads high, because your liberation is near"
(Luke 21:28).
But when God turns the tide, it doesn't happen without human
participation. Change, whether global, national, or within the life

of a community like the Church, is always a partnership between human beings and God.

I want us to listen today for some of the human ingredients necessary for God to turn the tide.

When God Turns the Tide, It Is Because There Are Those Who Stand for Truth

When Peter and the other apostles were dragged before the Sanhedrin, the Church had just been born and its message was not welcome. Public opinion was against them. They were followers of a person executed for blasphemy and crimes against the state, and they had already tasted one experience of prison.

These were heavy odds and the pressure to keep silence was strong. There was every reason to avoid controversy and to seek the anonymity of conventional opinion. Yet, here they were, arrested once more and back in the dock. And when they were berated for not keeping silence—for teaching in the name of Jesus and holding those who killed him accountable—Peter's reply was anything but conventional: *"We must obey God rather than men"* (Acts 5:30).

The die was cast. No more could any human being or human institution demand their highest allegiance. They stood their ground and stood for the truth.

The hinges upon which history swings are made of people like that.

On February second, I was at home watching the opening of Parliament, hoping for some small sign of movement toward change in our land. When President De Klerk made those dramatic announcements that opened the prison gates of despair, I stood still for a long time, transfixed and emotionally overwhelmed. Then I walked to our kitchen window. From there you can see a distant hill, and on that hill there stands a church where, back in the 1950s, a young priest once ministered to the people of a vibrant black township called Sophiatown. It was there that he tried to stop the military trucks that came in the night to take the people away and the bulldozers that smashed their houses down.

I looked out on the white suburb that rose on the ruins of Sophiatown. I remembered the final insult in the naming of that suburb, *Triomf.*[1] I remembered the little book written by that priest to expose *apartheid's* evil to the world, called *Naught for Your Comfort.*

The priest was admonished by his bishop and sent home to England. But he took with him his book to alert the world, and he left behind him a young black teenager who had been his altar boy and whom he had faithfully visited in the hospital when the boy had tuberculosis. The priest's name was Trevor Huddleston. The altar boy was Desmond Tutu. Huddleston's book may be dated now, but the altar boy is not. Huddleston's impact on South Africa through Desmond Tutu is immeasurable. There is a direct line between his witness in Sophiatown and this moment.

There have been many, many others who have stood for the truth. They have been a minority, but together, the convictions of that minority and their commitment to obey God and stand for God's truth have made it possible for this moment of God's intervention—God's turning of the tide.

Never underestimate the importance of ordinary people standing for the truth, because they also enable others to play their part.

For God to Turn the Tide, There Must Be Those Who Will Listen with Integrity

Peter's stand and his accusation that these people had done to death the Son of God caused uproar in the Sanhedrin. Like all people of power, they were enraged when their actions and motives were challenged. They determined right then to put the apostles to death.

But, at this dramatic moment, *"a member of the Council rose to his feet, a Pharisee called Gamaliel, a teacher of the law held in high regard by all the people"* (Acts 5:34), and his words too, helped God turn the tide.

For change to happen, we need not only those with courage to speak the truth but those who will listen with integrity. Gamaliel had no reason to like the apostles. He was a Pharisee, and the things Jesus taught were not good news for Pharisees. Yet, incredibly, he knew he must listen. Could they be right? And what if they were right? And in a moment, he was risking everything: the respect of his community, his status in the Sanhedrin, his future as a leader, to say:

> *Keep clear of these men, I tell you; leave them alone. For if this idea . . . of theirs is of human origin, it will collapse; but if it is from God, you will never be able to put them down, and you risk finding yourselves at war with God.* (Acts 5:38-39)

I believe that underlying the courageous speech made recently in the South African Parliament was a leader's fear of finding himself at war with God. President De Klerk had no reason to like those he set free that day; in his bones he must have known that his own position was doomed by doing so.

Certainly the pressures of economic sanctions and international isolation, of beleaguered borders and internal strife, have all played their part; but these things never moved his stubborn predecessor. Why did he make this giant leap? I have joked that De Klerk is our first literate president—that the writing has been on the wall for decades and that he is the first to be able to read it.

But more is involved here. Testimony to the moral and spiritual dimensions of De Klerk's decision comes from a surprising source. Joe Slovo, the leader of the South African Communist Party, is a man who has little time for religion, but listen to what he says: "My philosophy tells me that change is brought about by the forces of economic determinism, but this man had a Damascus Road experience. There is a moral basis for what he is doing."[2]

We do not know what happened to Gamaliel the Pharisee, and we do not know what will happen to De Klerk the leader of the *apartheid* government of South Africa. But each, in a singular and crucial moment of history, was used by God to turn the tide.

God's truth is advanced not only by those who proclaim it but by those who are willing to hear it. God calls for people who are big enough, leaders who are open, honest, and humble enough, to recognize truth even when it comes from despised Galileans, political prisoners, or humble priests.

So here are two ingredients needed for God to turn the tide:

- Peter says to the oppressed and silenced of the world: "You are not impotent. God is not with the big battalions. God is with the truth. Cleave to God's truth and love and justice and peace. Stand for it! Speak for it! That is all God asks."

- Gamaliel says to those in power: "Listen hard and carefully to the uncomfortable words and disturbing voices that come from below. Do not muzzle them, but hear them. Listen for what God may be saying through them. If you don't, you may find yourselves at war with God."

This story from Acts is a parable of our dialogue with God and the world. At times you may be called to be a Peter, standing against popular opinion at great cost. At other times you may need to be a Gamaliel, listening with integrity for God's word of warning.

And one more thing: This drama ends with both Peter and Gamaliel *trusting God with the consequences* of what they had done that day, with both showing a spirit that left space for the other— what we might call magnanimity.

After accusing his hearers of killing Jesus, Peter says that this very Jesus is *"leader and savior to grant Israel repentance and forgiveness of sins"* (Acts 5:31). In South Africa, in the midst of the toughest confrontations, those standing for the truth have said repeatedly to the white oppressors, "We oppose you in order to set you free from your racism and your prejudice and your fear."

After expressing his real doubts about the cause for which the apostles stood, Gamaliel says, in effect, "Why don't we leave the decision to God?" It would seem to me that De Klerk has, in a very real sense, opened up the future of our land, giving space for all to participate and for God to move.

The way was not easy from then on. The record in Acts of what happened after that makes very scary reading, and doubtless the days that lie ahead for us in South Africa will be fraught with risk. But God has turned the tide, and we can trust God with the consequences.

---

1. The Afrikaans word for "Triumph." The razing of Sophiatown was the first significant mass removal of black persons under *apartheid*. They were taken to a place called Meadowlands. This is how Soweto was born—out of dozens of forced removals like this.

2. As related to a journalist friend of mine at the time.

18

Proclaiming the Lord's Death—the Ongoing Cross

*When violence breaks out between African National Congress
and Inkatha supporters
Communion Service, August 19, 1990*

*Every time you eat this bread and drink this cup, you proclaim
the death of the Lord, until he comes. (1 Corinthians 11:26)*

This sermon was preached just days after Nelson
Mandela and F. W. de Klerk met in Pretoria and Mandela
announced the suspension of the "armed struggle."
Almost immediately, new forms of violence broke out, a
combination of state sponsored terrorism designed by
De Klerk's regime to sow murder and mayhem amongst
black political movements, and violent jockeying for
power between Mandela's African National Congress and
Chief Mangosuthu Buthelezi's Inkatha Movement. It
became clear that a new and terrible phase in South
Africa's agony was beginning. It ultimately claimed forty
thousand lives.

—∞—

Out of the carnage of the First World War, there came a book of poems written by Geoffrey A. Studdert-Kennedy, an Anglican chaplain who had struggled desperately to hold on to his faith in God and to share it with soldiers being slaughtered in the trenches. One of his poems is called simply, "The Suffering God." It explores some of the horrors he and his companions were facing each day, and some of the questions they raised about the kind of God who could permit all of this. The final verse reads:

> Father, if He, the Christ were Thy Revealer,
>   Truly the First-Begotten of the Lord,
> Then must Thou be a Suff'rer and a Healer,
>   Pierced to the heart by the sorrow of the sword.
>
> Then must it mean, not only that Thy sorrow
>   Smote Thee that once upon the lonely tree,
> But that to-day, to-night, and on the morrow,
>   Still it must come, O Gallant God, to Thee![1]

For Studdert-Kennedy, the only way to begin to understand the horrific suffering he had seen was that God, far from being a distant onlooker, was there in it all, *suffering too.* For him the cross was not only a "once for all" sacrifice—*it was a window into the heart of a God who continues to suffer with suffering people everywhere.*

I believe that.

Today I ask you to look at this Communion bread and this silver-plated chalice. Look deep into these symbols of Christ's suffering to the reality of a suffering God.

The apostle tells us that every time we eat of this bread and drink of this cup, we are announcing the death of Jesus again. We must do this until he comes. We are here because of Calvary, where Jesus died for us. We know that something happened there changing the equation between God and humankind forever. There, concretely and visibly, in human history, the Son of God offered himself up for us all.

It is done!

But we are here today also because Calvary is *never* done. In another sense, so long as the sin and hurt and violence and hate of humankind continues, so long is Jesus nailed to that cross. And we need to cry out! We need to proclaim with tears that *the death of the Lord is happening again, right here around us.* The cross is raised again, as it was long ago.

The Cross Was Raised by Those with Power, Determined Not to Let Go

Pontius Pilate, the Roman governor who sentenced Jesus to the cross, represented a system so accustomed to power that he could not imagine anything different. His life was determined by a culture of power. His station in life was measured by the amount of power in his own hands. He was in this grubby little part of the empire to preserve Rome's power and to advance his own. Pilate seems not to have been too interested in this young Rabbi until it affected the power equation. His unwillingness to crucify Jesus was plain—until his own power was threatened.

That is the way it always is.

The violence that has killed so many right here on our streets and in hostels nearby is part of an ongoing campaign by those in power in our land to hold grimly to their position. If they can divide, they can continue to rule.

They crucify again.

The Cross Was Raised by the Powerless Who Made Peace with Their Oppression

In the days of Jesus' death, the political story was so much like our own. The Sadducees and the Herodians, followers of King Herod, had determined that Roman rule was permanent and that the only future lay in proxy power. These were the "Homeland Leaders," the "Bantustan Rulers"[2] of Jesus' day. They were Rome's proxies, governing by permission and doing Rome's bidding.

If any change was to come to Palestine, they were the most threatened. They were among the few who had profited from oppression, and any threat to the status quo was a direct threat to their position.

If we look about us right now and ask who are the most threatened by liberation, it is not only the powerful whites but their black proxies. It is the surrogate rulers who have carved out positions of comfort and found themselves in a demonic alliance with this oppressive system.

Luke tells us that Herod and Pilate had had a long-standing feud until the trial of Jesus. Even then, they made the right political noises, arguing about jurisdiction; but underneath these power plays they knew that their interests coincided and finally, with Jesus' fate becoming increasingly certain, we are told, *"that same day, Herod and Pilate became friends"* (Luke 23:12).

What an evil day!

We need to be alert to similar alliances. The propaganda instruments of the system would have us believe that the deaths of innocent people right now are no more than a visitation of traditional tribal enmity—but we surely know better.[3]

Ask the simple question: Who are most threatened by the tide flowing towards freedom? Ask who stand to gain most from stemming this tide? Where are new friendships and alliances being forged? Why?

One thing is sure: The powerful and their surrogates have never hesitated to play their games with human lives, and we must never allow ourselves to accept such callousness.

The Cross Was Raised by People Whose Religion Served the Powerful

We should not forget that other main player in the manufacture of the cross. His name was Caiaphas, and he was the chief priest of the nation. Caiaphas might have been a good man, for all we know, and he may have had the interests of the people at heart; but in the drama of Jesus' death, it was Caiaphas who made the most blatantly political statement of all. He said, *"it is expedient that one man should die for the people."*

We need to face the fact that we, as Christians, have often lent our faith to the support of systems of power. When freedom comes, Christians in all churches, and some great denominations, will have to confess that they permitted, not one man, but hundreds of thousands of women, children, and men to die to keep their own kind in power. When the Reverend Frank Chikane was tortured, it was a member of his own denomination, the Apostolic Faith Mission, who was his torturer.[4]

Others of us have simply remained indifferent. That is what some would say is the real opposite of love: not hatred but indifference. We can be sure that not everyone was shouting insults at Calvary the day Jesus died. Most good citizens of Jerusalem were going about their business as if nothing extraordinary was happening at all. Their indifference allowed it all to happen. There is nothing new about that. Desmond Tutu says that it is impossible to wake up someone who is *pretending* to be asleep.

People of Faith Must See Deeper into This—and Proclaim the Lord's Death

The cross is raised by all these things: by the fear of losing power, by betrayal, by prostituted faith, by indifference; and if we are truly followers of Jesus, we cannot allow his murder to go unannounced. We are called to proclaim the Lord's death and to point to these complicities. *Right now it is our God who is being broken once more by our terrible deeds and chilling indifference.*

But there is something deeper. Every time we see a body lying in the street or by a railway track or at the door of a hostel, we need to hear the Christ crying, *"This is my body!" "This is my blood!"*

The cross was raised not only by humankind's sin. It was raised because God determined to come amongst us, to stand with us, to suffer with and for us. Jesus died not only as a victim but as a participant in something deep and profound.

"No one takes my life from me," he said, *"I lay it down of my own accord."*

He spoke openly of his coming death and said:

> *In very truth I tell you, you will weep and mourn, but the world will be glad. But though you will be plunged in grief, your grief will be turned to joy.* (John 16:20)

Christians have to come to the Lord's table with hope.

The first time this meal was ever shared, it was on the eve of the first Calvary. In their confusion, pain and fear, the disciples had little to feel hopeful about. It was only later, when he came again to them, bearing the wounds of his cross, that they knew the joy he had promised.

We must take this bread, this wine, and proclaim our gallant God's death yet again . . . until he comes.

He will come, as indeed will South Africa's Easter morning.

---

1. G. A. Studdert-Kennedy, *The Unutterable Beauty* (London: Hodder and Stoughton, 1927), p. 3.

2. The *apartheid* government set up a number of puppet black rulers in so-called tribal "homelands." Like puppet rulers throughout history, they were often even more ruthless than their masters in Pretoria.

3. The regime at this time was clearly backing and arming Buthelezi's Zulu-based Inkatha Movement, while selling the strife to the whites and the wider world as "Black-on-Black violence."

4. Dr. Frank Chikane succeeded Bishop Desmond Tutu as SACC General Secretary. Prior to this he had been detained without trial for his activism, and tortured.

19

What the Bomb Could Not Destroy

Opening of the new Khotso House,
headquarters of the South African Council of Churches
November 21, 1990

The pillar of cloud never left its place in front of the people by
day, nor the pillar of fire by night. (Exodus 13:23)

And so, King Agrippa, I was not disobedient to the heavenly
vision. (Acts 27:19)

The night of August 31, 1988, a team of secret police sabo-
teurs under Colonel Eugene De Kock, the notorious hit-
squad leader, planted explosives in the parking garage
under *Khotso*[1] House, the Johannesburg headquarters of the
South African Council of Churches. Just after midnight the
six-floor building was blasted so badly that it could never
be rebuilt. De Kock, who is serving a two hundred-year-
plus sentence for multiple assassinations, claims that the
orders to destroy the building came from the then state
president, P. W. Botha. On the afternoon following the
explosion, the minister of police, Mr. Adriaan Vlok, and
senior police generals, joined a celebratory barbecue at

De Kock's base. Vlok has since sought amnesty for his role in the bombing.

For two years, the SACC lived in diaspora, accommodated in various churches around the city. Then, through generous gifts from the world church community, a new Khotso House was purchased.

I had preached at the opening of the first Khotso House. It was a signal honor to do so at the dedication service of the second.

—∞—

As we dedicate this place to the glory of God and the service of the people, our minds are filled with memory. We recall the events since we opened the first *Khotso* House, and the people associated with that place. We remember moments of joy and pain, triumph and tragedy, hope and despair, anger and forgiveness.

I remember arriving outside that *Khotso* House in the small hours[2] of August 31, 1988, and being confronted by a scene from hell. The street littered with glass and masonry and twisted steel. Gaping window frames with shredded blinds fluttering like the tattered banners of a sacked fortress. Fires still burning in the basement, and where our foyer used to be, a yawning crater.

Amazingly, the Christ figure still hung on the foyer's rear wall. With the front of the building gone, it was exposed now to the street, arms outstretched over this ruination.

A Defining Moment in the History of Church and Land

That was a defining moment in the history of the Church and of this desperately loved and incredibly cruel land.

The history of the Church has been written in different ways.

- Sometimes it has been written in the declarations of its councils, like the Council of Jerusalem, where Christians first grappled with the spirit of exclusion that has cursed humankind—and almost destroyed South Africa. We have made our declarations too, like the "Message to the

People of South Africa," in 1968[3] that sustained the protest and resistance that has brought us to this day.

- Church history is also written in the life of each local community of believers where God longs to demonstrate an alternative, "Kingdom society." This Council strengthened the witness of many local congregations and gave courage to faint hearts. Our influence was not always as strong as we hoped, but the SACC could never be ignored.
- Church history is perhaps written most nobly in caring for God's people in the world—the little people, the suffering people for whom and among whom Christ died. We can be proud that through the long battle with evil, the doors of the SACC have always been open to countless wounded, scarred, and bereaved victims of *apartheid*.

Remember the statement issued by the SACC the day after the bomb?

> What was expressed in the day to day work in Khotso House was a determination by the vast majority of Christians in South Africa to end *apartheid* and establish God's justice. This determination cannot be destroyed and while we are under no illusions that this has been the last such attack upon us, we reaffirm that commitment today. The destruction of the "House of Peace" will in no way deter us from working for real peace.[4]

Symbol of God's Dream

Whether in bold acts of defiance, the challenging of our member Churches, or in binding up the broken victims, this Council of Churches is a symbol of God's dream of a new heaven and a new earth.

This chapel at the heart of the new *Khotso* House speaks of a community of God's people from different denominations, colors, cultures, and languages, who have been grasped by that dream and have tried to be faithful to it. Like Paul the apostle, we want to be able to say, "*I was not disobedient to the heavenly vision*" (Acts 26:19 RSV).

This place speaks of the true Church of Jesus Christ: to some in our land a scourge and a scandal, and to others, a beacon of hope in a deep, dark night.

Samuel Rayan says:

> A candle light is a protest at midnight.
> It is a non-conformist.
> It says to the darkness,
> "I beg to differ!"[5]

That is what this Council has been, a "protest at midnight."

Now the light is coming! The old South Africa is terminally ill. The new South Africa is going to be born. As we dedicate this place, we are on that journey in the wilderness that stands between Egyptian enslavement and the new land God wants to give us. How we behave and live on this journey will determine whether we arrive there, or—as often happens to those lost in the desert— find ourselves back where we started.

In some ways this journey will be more stressful than the days of captivity. The old South Africa has been oppressive, but at least we have known what to expect! Pharaohs are predictable! We have known what we were up against, what it could do to us, how to confront it, and sometimes blunt the worst of its blows. The journey to newness will be different. There are challenges on the road to God's new South Africa that we haven't begun to predict. We will need much courage and help from God each day.

In the Exodus, Yahweh sustained the desert sojourners with manna and gave them three gifts to keep them true. We are going to need these gifts, and South Africa is going to need them too.

An Enduring Vision

Yahweh did not leave the people without direction. Each dawn there appeared a cloudy pillar, and every night a flame glowed before them. God was leading them on.

We must faithfully hold before all our people God's unwavering dream of justice and *shalom*. Without that enduring vision on the horizon, calling us on and giving firm direction, we will soon be lost. Lest we forget the dream that sustained us in the long days of oppression, we must set our compasses by the guiding Spirit of God, who has led us thus far through prayer and struggle.

An Enduring Sense of God's Presence

Wherever they wandered, Israel's pilgrim people carried the Ark of the Covenant, placing it each night inside a Tabernacle in the center of their camp. When they were wandering in the desert, the weary sojourners must have often wanted to divest themselves of this heavy load. But they never did, because of Yahweh's solemn promise about the Ark and Tabernacle. *"It is there,"* Yahweh said *"that I shall meet you"* (Exodus 25:22).

The Ark gave them an enduring sense of the presence of God. It was to the Ark that the people looked in their need, and it was the Ark that they carried into battle. They knew that God was intimately among them.

If God's dream of a new land of justice and shalom is to come about, it will not be in our own strength, nor by our own wisdom. We must know that God wants to meet us, not on the periphery of events, but at the center of our camp. Only then can the Church in our day be an Ark of safety, where those who are battered and bruised and traumatized can find healing.

Enduring Values to Live By

Before they could enter Canaan, the people were held back at Sinai to learn that without new moral laws there could be no new land. Essential to their nation-building were the great ethical principles enshrined in the Torah.

Father Emmanuel Lafont reminded us recently, "God made his people wander for many years, in order to teach them not to behave like their former oppressors, but to be more human, more concerned, more communal in their life. God knew that otherwise freedom would have been just an empty shell."[6]

They were given a moral framework out of which they were to live, both individually and in community. A crucial task for the Church at this time will be to remind the emerging new South Africa of this framework.

The challenge is certainly daunting. *I suspect we will find that it was in some ways easier to resist evil than to give birth to the good, that we were better able to endure bondage than handle liberty.*

We may also find it was simpler to unmask *apartheid's* evil than to recognize its deformed stepchildren who will long be among us.

- One of them is hate, a drug that addicts not only oppressors but also many of the oppressed. There is urgent need to liberate people from hate addiction with the "expulsive power" of the love of God.

- Another is violence. *Apartheid* bred a culture of violence, and swords do not transform easily into ploughshares. That is why those committed to peacemaking are such crucial people right now in this land.

- Yet another is moral and legal anarchy. Where the law is a thief, breaking the law becomes a virtue. When we have ensured that the law becomes the people's friend, we will have to help a whole generation discover a new respect for the rule of law.

Seldom has the ethical content of the Christian faith been more critical, and the task of communicating it effectively is supremely that of the Church. We may not succeed in all of this, but we must do our best to be faithful. God has been faithful: Through all the desert years, God has been there.

All that God asks of us is that we may one day say, *"I was not disobedient to the heavenly vision."*

---

1. *Khotso:* Sesotho word for "Peace."

2. The Central Methodist Mission managed an apartment block for disability pensioners, Cornerstone House, immediately opposite *Khotso* House. Cornerstone House was badly damaged by the blast, and it was a call immediately afterward from its caretaker that brought Mr. John Rees and me to the scene first.

3. The "Message to the People of South Africa" was published by the South African Council of Churches over the signatures of numerous Church leaders and clergy, and distributed to all clergy in the major Churches. It represented the first of a series of significant declarations placing the Church in opposition to the State. The "Message" branded *apartheid* as trust in a false God.

4. Issued by the SACC on September 1, 1988.

5. These words by Samuel Rayan, a theologian from India, were sent to me in 1986 by a remarkable friend whom I met that year at the World Methodist Council meeting in Nairobi. Ann Bird and her family covenanted to light a candle and pray for Elizabeth and me each Sunday at their midday meal. They did this faithfully, sending a supportive card each week, until liberation came to South Africa. It was acts of solidarity such as these that held us strong.

6. Emmanuel Lafont was a Catholic priest from France, who lived in Soweto and was loved and trusted by the people of that massive township. His courage was legendary, and he was later decorated by the French government for his contribution to the South African liberation struggle. These words are from an address he gave at Regina Mundi Church, Soweto, at a "Nation-Building" service.

20

Living by the True Reality

Prayer Vigil the night before Alan Storey's Trial
April 14, 1991

The issue of compulsory military service faced each of our sons, as it did every white male youth in South Africa. It is a cruel thing to ask mere teenagers to struggle with the complex issues of peace and war, violence and nonviolence, the more so in an atmosphere soaked with propaganda and massive state pressure.[1]

John and Christopher, our eldest sons, had obeyed their initial military call-up, serving in the South African Navy. Happily, they were never involved in direct military encounters with fellow South Africans fighting for liberation. After completing their two years, they determined to disobey any further call-ups, and did so. Our third son, David, was a university student, able by law to have his call-up deferred, until he declared himself an objector in late 1990.

Alan, our youngest, was in a more vulnerable position. While still at school, he had decided never to serve in apartheid's military machine, and was also thinking of entering the Christian ministry. After leaving South Africa for a year to struggle with his vocation and deepening pacifist convictions, he returned to enter the Church's on-the-job training system. This left him exposed to the call-up. He

entered a very lonely period assisting the minister of a conservative white rural congregation, where neither offered
any support for his stand.

On the due day, I accompanied him to hand himself over
for arrest, his trial date was set, and he began to prepare for
six long years in prison. The Methodist Order of
Peacemakers and the anti-conscription movement in
Johannesburg rallied wonderfully. Posters appeared all
over the city publicizing his witness, and he was encouraged by other objectors who had gone this costly way
before him.

This reflection was offered at the Prayer Vigil in CMM's
Chapel, held the night before his trial began.

It was not easy to preach.

—␣␣—

Alan Walker tells the story of a young conscientious objector
standing before a Russian tribunal during the 1914–1918 War. The
lad had declared that he was a Christian, and that the laws of the
Kingdom of God forbade him to kill. The magistrate, acknowledg-
ing the boy's sincerity, said, "Your stand against conscription
would be more understandable if this 'Kingdom' of which you
speak, had come already." The young man answered simply, *"For
me, the Kingdom of God has come."*[2]

It was the Velveteen Rabbit who asked the Skin Horse (who "was
so old that his brown coat was bald in patches and showed the seams
underneath, and most of the hairs in his tail had been pulled out"),

"What is REAL?" . . .

"Real isn't how you are made," said the Skin Horse. "It's a
thing that happens to you. When a child loves you for a long, long
time, not just to play with, but REALLY loves you, then you
become Real."

"Does it hurt?" asked the Rabbit.

"Sometimes," said the Skin Horse, for he was always truthful.
"When you are Real you don't mind being hurt."[3]

This Prayer Vigil is about what it means to be real. It is about *living by the true reality.*

Many will say that the stand taken by Alan Storey is an unrealistic one. They will say that because we live in a fallen and imperfect world, there will be times when it is necessary to use violent methods like killing people to defend the good and defeat the bad. That is one view of what is real. Its starting point is the reality of evil and it builds from that point.

Others, however, will say that our starting point must go beyond the reality of evil *to the greater reality of God*. We must build our thinking from that place where Jesus met evil and overcame it—at the cross.

We know that when most people look at Christ on the cross, they see something foolish and something weak; but for us it is there that we see true reality—*God's way of confronting evil with radical, suffering love*. This is the reality that Alan lives by, and that is why he cannot lend his support to the unrealistic and outworn way of violence.

His witness is especially important to South Africa at this time because we are living in a land that has surrendered itself to violence. South Africa is learning that if you justify violence for *any* reason, no matter how good and noble, you legitimize it for *every* reason, no matter how wrong and unworthy. We are reaping the bitter fruit of that justification. Weapons once dedicated to liberty are now being used for thuggery, and those who use them don't care about the difference.

The only way for our land to be set free from this terrible cycle is for a growing number of people to recognize the tragic betrayal that comes from this trust in force. More and more people need to discover the new reality that Alan stands for. He is going further than saying, "I won't use violence to defend *apartheid*." He is saying, "I could not use violence even to destroy it." His stand is a challenge not only to *apartheid*'s conscription system but also to that other, equally evil practice which forces people into violent actions in the townships in the name of liberation or party loyalty or ideological dominance. His stand is a radical break with using violence as a means of dealing with any dispute. He really believes that:

> When anyone is united to Christ, there is a new world; the old order has gone, and a new order has already begun.
> (2 Corinthians 5:17)

That is why, although we feel much pain at what might happen to him, tonight is a celebration of God's new reality; the Kingdom

of justice and peace which Jesus said we must seek before everything else is already amongst us in this act of witness. We can be
joyful because Alan has discovered what it is to be real. He knows
what it is to be loved, to love, and to refuse not to love—even
though "it might hurt sometimes." As the Skin Horse said to the
Velveteen Rabbit, "When you are real, you don't mind being hurt,"
and, "Once you are real, you cannot become unreal again."

I pray that many, many others will find the strength to stand
where Alan stands. Only then will a truly new South Africa be
possible.

Postscript

Later, amazingly we did see a sign of that new South
Africa. Alan's trial began, only to be interrupted when the
prosecutor asked for a postponement. No date was set, he
was released without bail, and has never been called back.
He was the last conscientious objector to be tried, and the
next military call-up was a failure. Conscription had effectively ended in South Africa.

Many influences had brought this about: opposition by
the SACC and the South African Catholic Bishops'
Conference, the determination of groups such as the End
Conscription Campaign, the Conscientious Objectors'
Support Group, and the Conscientious Objection Advice
Offices.

More than anything, however, conscription ended
because of the costly witness of numbers of remarkable
young men who were willing to go to prison or suffer
calumny for their principles. Alan was the last in this long
line.

---

1. The penalty for refusing to undergo military service was six years' imprisonment. The penalty for "advising or encouraging" conscientious objection was five
years' imprisonment.

2. The Reverend Alan Walker, preaching at the World Methodist Peace
Conference, Wesley's Chapel, London, July, 1985.

3. Margery Williams, *The Velveteen Rabbit: Or How Toys Become Real* (Boston:
David R. Godine, 1983), pp. 4-6.

21

Let God Be God!

The Call for a Kingdom People
Lake Junaluska, North Carolina, 1989

I am the Lord; the Lord is my name; I will not give my glory to another God. (Isaiah 42:8)

Set your minds on God's kingdom and his justice before anything else. (Matthew 6:33)

Through all the bad years in South Africa, one joyful privilege was to preach internationally. These journeys, about twice a year, were opportunities to breathe the air of freedom. They were also important in building and retaining the solidarity of the world Church, something very precious to us in the struggle. We will never be able to repay our Christian friends across the world for their constancy in prayer and action. The engagement of the world Church in South Africa's agony provides a model for new possibilities of Christian action in the name of God's compassion and justice in other parts of the earth.

Different versions of this sermon were preached in Britain, Germany, Scandinavia, Australia, the United States, and in Asia. This is the American version.

—⚏—

Two thousand years ago a young Jewish carpenter began to preach in Galilee. At the heart of his message was the call for a rebel world to return to its rightful ruler: "The time has come," he said, "The Kingdom of God is upon you! Repent and believe the Gospel." From the beginning of his ministry to its end, Jesus of Nazareth spoke of the Kingdom. Urgently, passionately, he called his hearers to make this their one priority.

"Set your minds on God's kingdom and his justice before everything else."

If we name the name of Jesus, clearly this is what we ought to be doing. Seeking the Kingdom of God must take first place. It must be our supreme allegiance. There can be no other. The followers of Jesus in every age and on every continent must be "Kingdom people," bearers of the Kingdom dream.

In my land, South Africa, over the last forty years, no message has been more important for the Church. It should be no different in this more fortunate land.

Who are these Kingdom people? What do they believe? How do they live?

The Kingdom People Will Let God Be God, and the Church Be the Church

In the dark 1930s, a new idolatry swept Germany and millions began raising their arms in salute to Adolf Hitler, and when Christian leaders also began to bow to this demagogue, a great theologian, Karl Barth, stood up and cried, *"Let God be God!"* We need to hear that cry again, for just as most Germans allowed the lines between faith and ideology to become blurred and indistinct, we can do the same.

In South Africa, the pagan notion of racial purity and pride has become the nation's god and that sick and false religion stains everything we do.

- And here? Is it possible that in this most prosperous and powerful nation on earth, prosperity and power have blinded people to the supremacy of the living God?

Let me warn now that God won't stand for this. God says, *"I am the Lord, the Lord is my name. My glory I will not give to another."* God refuses to change places with anything or anyone.

Let God be God!

But this means that the Church must be the Church! Jesus brought into being an entirely new, radically different community, offering people a citizenship transcending the frontiers of nations and contrasting powerfully with the norms around it. The Church is not simply another institution in society, nor is it an extension of the traditions of any nation.

One of the great tragedies of my home, South Africa, is that some parts of the Christian Church have become the mouthpiece, not of God but of the state.

- And here? Where good and evil are mixed into a much more subtle blend? To what degree do Christians here think that the Gospel is just the religious face of the American way of life?

The Church must be different from, and often over against and in contradiction to, the ways of all nations. That alternative identity must be cherished and guarded as the most important characteristic of the Church. *The richest gift the Church can give the world is to be different from it.* It must be a constant irritant that the world doesn't want, but cannot do without.

In South Africa, other Christians have said no to the false gods of race and pride and placed the Church on a collision course with the state. We are now locked in a long and costly struggle, but in the midst of it we have been given a precious gift. When we were cast out of the corridors of power and disowned and vilified by the state, at first we saw it as a loss of influence. But in that loss we found our souls and rediscovered our identity. We were set free from the false patriotism that worships the nation's idols. We found instead a higher patriotism that determined to hold the nation accountable to the Kingdom of God and God's justice before everything else.

- And here? Things may be different, but I confess to a deep discomfort at having to preach in such close proximity to your national flag. At home in South Africa, the

Methodist Church has banned flags, any flags, from our sanctuaries. You see, our national flag is stained by deeds of which we are deeply ashamed—by our national sin. Perhaps yours is not, although I wonder if there are any unstained national banners? Whatever you feel about your flag, however, the important thing is *that its proximity to this pulpit might cause people to confuse their nation with their God* and the national interest with the purposes of God—and that is idolatry.

Whenever you are tempted to get too excited about your nation, remember that in giving birth to Israel, God expressly forbade any national symbol at all. Remember that there will be no national emblems in heaven. In the vision of John in Revelation, he saw no flags. Instead, the symbols of nationalism were gone, and in their place

> . . . *a vast throng, which no one could count, from every nation, of all tribes, peoples and languages, standing in front of the throne and before the Lamb. They were robed in white and had palms in their hands, and they shouted together: "Victory to our God who sits on the throne, and to the lamb."* (Revelation 7:9, 10)

Let God be God—then the Church will be the Church.

Kingdom People Will Engage the World with a Whole Gospel

Jesus commands us to engage the world. He said, *"Go into all the world."* (Matthew 28:19). Go into the world of leisure, economics and politics, human relationships and conflicts, to be agents of transformation, proclaiming:

> *Good news to the poor,*
> *Release for prisoners,*
> *Recovery of sight for the blind,*
> *To let the broken victims go free . . .*
> *And proclaim the year of the Lord's favour.*
> (Luke 4:18-19)

To obey this command, we must go with the *whole* Gospel of Christ, not some amputated portion of it.

There is a sterile debate we need to end:

- On the one hand, there are those who see the Gospel as internal and personal only. For such people the Kingdom reaches no further than the conversion of the individual soul. Their God is too small to transform the world.
- On the other hand, there are those who see the Gospel only in secular and political terms. For such people the struggle to transform society is all that matters. Their God is too busy to heal a wounded soul.

They label each other and abuse each other, each claiming that their half of the Gospel is all there is. They are like two castaways on a desert island. The one has the can of food, the other has the can opener—and each thinks that life depends on him alone! We should have nothing to do with this absurd and unbiblical debate.

We need a "prophetic evangelism." We need to be evangelical enough to know that evil begins in the unredeemed soul, and we must call for conversion; but we must be prophetic enough to know that evil expresses itself most malevolently when it penetrates our corporate life, where we have learned to let our institutions do our sinning for us—so we must work for social transformation and justice.

Only a whole Gospel is big enough to address both dimensions of need in this world.

Kingdom People Will Be Servant People

Much that passes for Christian thinking today is as concerned with health, wealth, and happiness as any television commercial—and hardly distinguishable from such values. Popular religion has bought into this ladder-climbing search for wealth, comfort, and power.

How difficult it is for us to remember that we follow a country carpenter who had no place to lay his head! One of the ironies of today is that secular institutions are discovering that the servant lifestyle of Jesus has important lessons for them, while the church of Jesus tends more and more to resemble a bloated business enterprise, run by managers rather than ministers—servants.

Not so Jesus. For him, servanthood is the authentic expression of Kingdom living

Dick Georgiades is credited with turning British Airways round from a money loser to the most profitable airline in the world. When asked the secret of this achievement, he said it was really quite simple. "We just turned our management philosophy upside down," he said, " and *everyone became accountable to the person below them, rather than the one above them.*" Here is a massive corporation embracing the servant lifestyle of Jesus! The focus of the entire organization ended up being the humble passenger in economy class, instead of the top executive.

Who is the focus of the Church? Who is the person we are concerned about? The person we exist to serve? For Jesus there was no question. In the Kingdom, the humble are lifted high and the most vulnerable have pride of place. That is why you cannot ask Jesus into your heart alone. He will ask, *"Can I bring my friends?"* You will look at his friends and they will consist of poor and marginalized and oppressed, and you will hesitate. But Jesus is clear: "Only if I can bring my friends."

Ask yourself which Christian has most powerfully impacted the imagination and conscience of the modern world. A satin-suited, prosperous televangelist? Or a wizened old Albanian nun, who made herself the servant of the poorest of the poor, the dying people of Calcutta?

Kingdom People Will be Messengers of Peace

Kingdom living is about who and what we trust. The Church's deepest compromise, and its most long-standing act of disobedience, has yet to be faced. In the nineteenth century, the Church came to grips with slavery; in the twentieth century, we finally recognized and repudiated colonialism and racism and began to deal with some of our other historical exclusions. Is it too much to hope that in the twenty-first century the Church will finally recognize, repent of, and repudiate our collaboration with war?

The so-called "Just War" theory is threadbare—I cannot think of one conflict in my lifetime that met all of its criteria. Even the Second World War that profoundly impacted my childhood and is offered as the great contest with evil, fails some of those criteria. Ask the Polish people, on whose behalf Britain supposedly first went to war, whether it resulted in their freedom or further enslavement? Ask the Jews, who lost six million people in the Holocaust, whether their suffering was at any time a significant priority for the Allies?

We have to choose the ground upon which we are going to stand. We have to determine what will pass away and what will endure. We have to decide which has the most reality for us: the reality of human sin and the fallenness of this world or the efficacy of Christ's cross. Of the cross, the apostle Paul says that he preached *"so that the fact of Christ on his cross might have its full weight"* (1 Corinthians 1:17). He goes on to declare that:

> *This doctrine of the cross is sheer folly to those on their way to ruin, but to us who are on the way to salvation it is the power of God.* (1 Corinthians 1:18-19)

Kingdom people must ultimately decide for what he calls the "foolishness of the cross" against what the world calls wisdom. It is surely time to forsake the tired logic of humankind that has brought us nothing but war and death for so long—and embrace the absurdity of a crucified God.

The ultimate choice before God's Kingdom people, is between the world's understanding of wisdom and power, and the apparent foolishness and weakness of the cross. When we sing, "Lift high the cross!" we are choosing that apparent foolishness and weakness. Jesus refused to see any person as enemy; he refused to believe peaceful ends could be gained by violent means; he refused to use violence to overthrow even evil.

It's time for us to embrace his most costly teaching. Nothing else will bring true *shalom*.

Kingdom People Will Seek Not to Be Successful, But Faithful

It's all very well to say we worship a carpenter who lived simply, who influenced only a small handful of followers, and who died on a cross; but we all want to be successful. The problem is that there are times, as Jesus found, *when you cannot be both faithful and successful*. This is a hard lesson to learn.

When I was appointed to Central Methodist Church in Johannesburg in 1976, arguably the premier Methodist pulpit in the land, I was deeply aware of the privilege. But Central Church was exclusively white; and I was convinced that unless that changed, this great pulpit could have nothing to say to the land of *apartheid*. The commitment to integrate our congregation was accepted by some remarkable people among the lay leaders, as it was rejected by others. In the end, after walkouts and protests from the reactionaries, we became a congregation that wonderfully and joyfully modeled the new South Africa God was trying to bring to birth. But two hundred white members had left us.

Success? That surely is not the right word. It was a journey of painful faithfulness that hurt every step of the way. The important thing, however, is that when the 1980s came, with their terrible years of oppression and polarization, this congregation was prepared. As separation, alienation, and war divided our land even more, this congregation became a sign of hope—*a promise of God's future*. This is because, when it was least popular, we determined to stand on Kingdom ground. Central to that stand was the conviction that Jesus died for *all*, that *all* are fellow citizens with God's people, and *all* are no longer strangers. The congregation is not as large as it once was. I have no idea how big it might have become had we not made that stand, but if we had not, I would be ashamed to face you today.

That congregation has, time and again, been my inspiration in a long struggle. A treasured possession is a photograph of them taken one Sunday morning. There, in a busy arcade in the center of Johannesburg, is this amazing community—brown, black, and white. They are a lovely splash of rainbow in a society obsessed with being white.

Successful? The word doesn't belong in the Christian's lexicon. Faithful? Ah, yes! That is what we must ask ourselves everyday.

These Then Are Some of the Criteria of a Kingdom People

They will truly be the Church, because they are determined to let God be God. They will proclaim a Gospel big enough for both personal salvation and social transformation. They will live the servant way and be messengers of peace. And they will seek simply to be faithful, trusting God with the rest.

Why am I saying "they"? Surely I should be saying "we"!

22

Letting Go of Privilege

Bedfordview Methodist Church, Johannesburg
Holy Week, 1994

Let your bearing towards one another arise out of your life in
Christ Jesus. For the divine nature was his from the first; yet he
did not think to snatch at equality with God, but made himself
nothing, assuming the nature of a slave. Bearing the human like-
ness, revealed in human shape, he humbled himself, and in obedi-
ence accepted even death—death on a cross. Therefore God raised
him to the heights and bestowed on him the name above all
names, that at the name of Jesus every knee should bow—in
heaven, on earth, and in the depths—and every tongue confess,
"Jesus Christ is Lord," to the glory of God the Father.
(Philippians 2:5-11)

The first democratic elections in South Africa's long and
bloody history were about to take place. Right-wing
extremists were planting bombs and vowing to fight to the
last, and most white people were certainly apprehensive. It
was important to help white Christians think theologically
about the changes required of them. That meant, among
other things, confronting the need for sacrifice, and seeing
the new challenges from the perspective of the Gospel. It
was also important that they learn to celebrate their liberation from the role of oppressor. They too were being
offered new life by South Africa's transition to freedom.

This sermon was preached to an affluent white congregation in Johannesburg's suburbs, as part of a Holy Week series on "Risking the Way of Jesus."

—⚒—

The crucifixion of Jesus began long before he was born. It began in eternity, with a decision in the heart of God to journey from glory into poverty, from power to vulnerability, from awesomeness to nothing. The God of all the universe made a conscious decision to *journey downwards*, to be born as a human baby in a finite world.

Marveling at this amazing journey, the apostle Paul says:

For the divine nature was his from the first; yet he did not think to snatch at equality with God, but made himself nothing, assuming the nature of a slave. Bearing the human likeness, revealed in human shape, he humbled himself, and in obedience accepted even death—death on a cross. (Philippians 2:5-8)

What does the hymn writer say?

> He laid His glory by,
>   He wrapped Him in our clay; [and]
> Our God contracted to a span, [a human life span]
>   incomprehensibly made man.[1]

That was the first step to Calvary; what theologians call the *kenosis* or self-emptying of God. Calvary begins with the willing and loving release of privilege and power. The salvation of your soul and the salvation of the world begins with the letting go of privilege—by none other than your God!

—⚒—

This Holy Week comes during significant days in the history of our land. We are preparing for changes that many have suffered and died to see come about, and that others still fiercely resist. They will be the most radical changes in all the sad years that are South Africa. Whatever else they will bring, these changes will confront all white South Africans with an inescapable challenge. We must learn from Jesus *how to let go of privilege.*

It's Hard to Let Go

The privileged and the powerful in South Africa are being called to let go—that's the heart of what all this change is about, isn't it—but the letting go of privilege is very hard. We look at somebody like Lucas Mangope and we say, "Why didn't he have the sense to bow out gracefully? Couldn't he read the signs and get out while the going was good? If he had done that, people would not have died in Mmabatho and Mafikeng."[2] True, but when we have power and privilege, they become very dear to us and it is never easy to let go.

I remember discovering this in myself when flying with a group of South African Church leaders to Europe and the United States. At Johannesburg airport, we were surprised to discover that we were booked in business class. I had never traveled business class before—in fact the thought of a Christian minister traveling anything other than economy was unacceptable to me; but our overseas hosts had done the booking, and they obviously had a different view. We couldn't argue about it, could we? Well, it was wonderful! The seats were wide, you could tip them back, your feet came up in front of you, and the cabin crew kept bringing all sorts of nice tidbits. It was very, very nice indeed; and by the time we got to Amsterdam, I was getting used to being pampered and spoiled!

At Amsterdam we had to change for the leg to New York, and while we were waiting, just four of us heard our names announced. We responded, and found an apologetic KLM spokesperson who said, "We are so sorry but your aircraft to New York has engine trouble, and we've had to replace it with another one. The replacement has a different seating configuration, a smaller business class, so we hope you don't mind traveling economy to New York? We've given you each two seats to try and make up for it." Now I should have been grateful to revert to my more appropriate and humble image, but I wasn't. Truth be told, I was fed up! I found myself wondering why I had to be one of the unfortunate four. Didn't I look like business class material? And what was so special about the others who hadn't been bumped down to economy? Ten hours of business class travel had weaned me quite effectively from my humility.

Letting go of privilege—any form of privilege—is hard, and if you are a white South African, you have shared in the power and the privilege of our *apartheid* past. Don't tell me you haven't done as well as the next person because it's hardly relevant. If you are white like me, *that accident of birth ensured that you and I have traveled business class all our lives.* I'm not saying that we are bad people, nor that we are necessarily racist people. We were just born into it, we got used to it, and because we now take it for granted, letting go will be hard.

But a lot of letting go is going to have to happen. Some will cost us materially as we seek to correct the inequities of *apartheid*, but even more difficult will be *the internal letting go of long-held attitudes and assumptions* that must happen in our souls.

Letting go is very hard, and we will need the help of Jesus.

It Begins with Identification

When I read about Jesus, I see that letting go begins with identification—a very scary word. Identification is more than just caring or feeling for people. Identification is becoming one with people, *it is risking your identity by sharing the identity of another.*

When the Nazis invaded Denmark in the Second World War, notices soon went up in Copenhagen, ordering all Jews to sew big yellow Stars of David to their clothes so everybody could identify them as Jews—as a lower form of life. King Christian of Denmark was in the habit of riding in the parks of Copenhagen every day; and the day after that edict was published, he went for his ride as usual. Just one thing was different. *Sewn to his tunic, for everybody to see, was a large yellow Star of David.*

Father Damien was chaplain to the leper colony on Molokai Island. He tried to care for the lepers, he preached to them as best he might, and he loved them. But there was always that distance between these people whose bodies were being eaten up and somebody whose flesh was whole. One day, when Father Damien was preparing food in his little kitchen, some boiling water fell on his foot, and to his surprise he felt no pain. He looked more closely and saw the dreaded signs of leprosy. After staring for a long time at this evidence that should have devastated him, he ran from his house and up the hill to the little chapel, and began to ring the bell so wildly that all the lepers on the island hurried there. When they had gathered, Father Damien stood up in front of them with tears pouring down his cheeks, and yet with a glorious smile, and then he greeted them: *"Fellow lepers! Fellow lepers!"*

At Bethlehem in Judea, some two thousand years ago, the God and the King of the Universe donned the badge of our humanity and cried out from a little manger, *"Fellow human beings!"* That great *kenosis* was God passionately identifying with us.

When love fills you with the joy of being one with those who are less fortunate than you, that is identification. If we try to get into the shoes of those who have nothing, we will be less obsessive about wanting everything. If you are struggling with what letting go will require of you, remember that the closer you get to those who are hurting and those who have suffered and those who have been broken by this land, the less difficult it will be for you.

Identification helps begin the letting go.

Our Priorities Change

When we begin to identify with the pain of the people in this land, it will change what is important to us. Have you noticed that from the start of his ministry right until Calvary, Jesus turned the values of society upside down—or shall I say, the right way up? Because he became one with the least and lowest in his world, he always saw things through different eyes.

Someone has said that life is like a shop window where somebody has broken in at night and exchanged all the price tags so that the things that are really cheap have been marked most expensive and things that are really valuable are now marked dirt cheap. That's what life has done; that's what society does. Something has to happen in us to get our values right again.

An encounter with a life-threatening illness will do it. I was fortunate. I had a "heart attack" in London, which later turned out to be something else, but I was not to know that at the time. When I collapsed, the ambulance took me to hospital, and I woke up in the Intensive Care Unit with a doctor leaning over me saying, "You've had a heart attack." That kind of news concentrates the mind! You lie there thinking, and you realize that the time you've got to live is probably much more limited than you imagined. The way you're going to live it would have to change. The things you thought were important (I was rushing through London to catch a connection to New York to speak at an important conference, and what I was going to say was so *very* important!) recede from your mind. Other priorities came to the fore, like my relationships, the people I loved, the way I was spending my time, and how ready I was to meet my God. All of these things suddenly became very important. (I confess however, that thirty-six hours later, when they told me, "You haven't had a heart attack after all," I got the first taxi I could to Heathrow, flew to New York and managed to deliver my lecture after all. I'm a very slow learner, but don't let that spoil the point I'm making!)

I'm not recommending illness, but I am saying that we will find it easier to let go privilege if we think differently about what's important.

We have to decide in this land whether we are followers of Jesus, who had nowhere to lay his head but knew what was really important—the needs of that leper, that poor person, that broken woman, that sinner. Are we followers of that leader? Or do we follow the leaders who are even now bickering about who is going to have what slice of which territory and are willing for their followers to hack people to death to get it? How many more people must die for their ambitions?

Letting Go Brings Life

Jesus once spoke these incredible words, *"Whoever would save his life shall lose it, but whoever shall lose his life for my sake and the gospel's shall save it"* (Mark 8:35). This is the same Jesus who said, *"I have come so that you may have life, life in all its fullness"* (John 10:10).

Clearly, what Jesus calls life is very different from what we call success. That's what the encounter between Jesus and the young man who we call the "rich young ruler" was about. He had money, he had power, he had everything that we call success; yet Jesus says to this young man, "Why don't you go and sell all of that stuff, and then come and follow me." Why would Jesus say that? Is it because he had a particularly negative approach to people who were lucky enough to be rich? I don't think so. If Jesus just intended to put this young man in his place, he would not have looked upon him with sorrow as he walked away. No, Jesus was saying to this young man, *"Friend, I want to set you free. I want to liberate you from your bondage to privilege and wealth so that you may find real life."*

I don't know whether we who have been privileged in this country know how imprisoned we are. The possessions that come with privilege often hold us hostage. It may be, now we are asked to give up some things, that we will know freedom for the first time by letting them go. Power and privilege will pass and fade and perish. Real life is about something else.

I have a delightful modern summary of the Bible called *Manna and Mercy*, and in one of the pages of this little book, the writer wants to tell us what happened when people met Jesus. Note that he has taken every word straight out of the Gospel record.

> Lepers, prostitutes, tax collectors, sinners, poor people, discarded ones, blind people, debtors, outcasts, children, women, men, elderly people, sick people, Gentiles, Samaritans, Jews, demon-possessed people, outsiders, heretics, Pharisees, lawyers, and even rich people and big deals were . . .
>
> invited, included, affirmed, loved, touched, liberated, held, embraced, healed, cleansed, given dignity, fed, forgiven, made whole, called, reborn, given hope, received, honored, freed.[3]

That's what happened when Jesus was around. Not a single person excluded, not a single grace held back. That's what life is about—life in all its fullness.

And so we come to the cross, where Jesus let go everything for love. And we who find it so difficult to let go stand in awe because that place of dying to self becomes a place of profound beauty and joy, the place where we find life. And this Jesus who humbled himself even to death on a cross, is the one whom God has raised to the heights bestowing on him the name above all names, that at the name of Jesus every knee should bow—in heaven, on earth, and in the depths—and every tongue confess, "Jesus Christ is Lord," to the glory of God the Father.

When you come near to the cross this Holy Week, risk letting go.

1. Charles Wesley, "Let earth and heaven combine," *The Methodist Hymn-Book* (London: Methodist Conference Office, 1933), no. 142.

2. Mangope was president of Bophutatswana, one of the artificial "Bantu Homelands" set up by the *apartheid* regime. Even when *apartheid* began to collapse, he assumed he could continue to rule his mythical republic. He was rudely ousted and some lives were lost in the action.

3. Daniel Erlander, *Manna and Mercy—A Brief History of God's Unfolding Promise to Mend the Entire Universe* (Mercer Island, Wash.: The Order of Saints Martin and Teresa, 1992), p. 45 (format changed).

23

Celebration at the District Six Plaque of Conscience

Buitenkant Street Methodist Church,
District Six, Cape Town
Sunday, November 1, 1992

The gates of the city shall never be shut by day—and there will
be no night. (Revelation 21:25)

The bulldozing of District Six was one of the most vicious of apartheid's acts of cruelty. Situated on the slopes of Table Mountain, District Six was Cape Town's most colorful and integrated residential area. It was the home of lower income, mixed-race people. In 1966 the regime declared District Six to be a "White Group Area," effectively sentencing its more than thirty thousand inhabitants to forced removal over the next few years. I ministered in District Six from 1967 to 1972 and in spite of the protests we mounted, had to see one family after another lose their home and be carried away to dreary rows of "matchbox" houses fifteen miles away.

In 1971 our congregation determined that this monstrous evil had to be marked in some way. Out on the street, directly opposite Cape Town's main police station, we placed an engraved plaque on our church wall. After a service of protest and prayer in the sanctuary, we went into the street to dedicate it. The Plaque of Conscience on the wall of Buitenkant Street Methodist Church, District Six, was South Africa's first public memorial to the horrors of *apartheid,* and it survived much abuse until freedom came. Today, the church with its plaque has become the District Six Museum, visited by thousands of people from all over the world each year.

This sermon, incorporating much of what I preached at the original Dedication in 1971, was to celebrate of the end of *apartheid,* and the news that the original inhabitants of District Six would be able to return and rebuild.

It may also serve as an end to this collection, a reminder of the biblical certainty that held us throughout the decades of struggle in South Africa, and which must inform and challenge our future.

Twenty-one years ago, many of you here today gathered in this same sanctuary to strike a small blow against a monstrous evil. We dedicated a simple brass plaque to stand testimony to our anger and pain. The plaque read:

ALL WHO PASS BY

Remember with shame the many thousands
of people who lived for generations
in District Six and other parts of
this city and were forced by law to
leave their homes because of the
colour of their skins.

FATHER, FORGIVE US

Today we need to remember that time. We need to be reminded of the awesome power of the *apartheid* state. We need to recall that people were so terrified of that power that we could not at first find an engraver willing to make a plaque with those words on it, and when we did, it was on condition that we never named the engraving firm! In its first month, it was ripped off and then defaced. After that they tolerated it—after all, they ruled the land and their bull-dozers were already laying this place waste.

Let me read you parts of the sermon I preached twenty-one years ago:

> We come in sadness and shame: shame that human com-passion has been blinded by ideology and that the gods of racial purity can be more important than the God who makes us all one family. But we do not come in a spirit of dumb resignation. Rather let there be a quiet confidence among us that such things shall come to an end. The time will come when such iniquities as this plaque reminds us of will be a repudiated, repented past.
>
> But if that is to happen, reminders there must be. If that is to happen, none must be allowed to walk at ease. Let none become comfortable in the presence of this terrible thing. Let none pretend it didn't happen. All who pass by, remember with shame!
>
> The test of any legislation is what it does to people—ordi-nary people who are precious in the sight of God. It is the flesh and blood behind the statistics that count. No glib talk of "separate freedoms"—no amount of paternalistic talk—can disguise or shut out the cry that there is being perpe-trated here a monstrous evil. When the list of humanity's heartlessness is read, history will judge the Group Areas Act[1] as among the most heartless and destructive.

I remember speaking of the people who would suffer:

> It is the residents of Hanover and De Villiers Streets, of Vernon Terrace, Drury Lane and William Street and Lavender Hill—the more than thirty thousand people who have called District Six "home"—who bear the immediate consequences of this crime. Malay and Christian and Jew, rich and poor, light and dark, Afrikaans and English speak-ing, these are the people who are being banished daily to the inhospitable wastes of the Cape Flats.

I spoke of the economic hardships and also of the broken hearts, of the old man who came on a rainy day to ask me to bury his wife.

"Soon after the Group came and moved us," he said, "she died of a broken heart." I conducted his own funeral hardly a month later.

I also spoke of the white people of Cape Town and the price they would pay in their souls:

> As whites place those we hurt beyond our city walls where they are no longer visible, we are cutting ourselves off from our consciences and sealing ourselves into our own ghetto of indifference. '*All you who pass by . . . remember with shame!*'

So it was a dark day. But the darkness was not absolute:

> We dedicate this plaque also in hope. We meet in pain and anger, but not in defeat. We meet here in confidence because God will not allow *apartheid* to live forever. The wall of partition being so cruelly built at this time will be broken down by our Christ. The tears that so many shed today will one day be wiped dry.
>
> Until that day, no matter how many people and families are moved, none will be able to remove the spirit of District Six out of our hearts; and whatever happens to the buildings and streets around this church, let us commit ourselves to preserve this place.
>
> Let it stand as a sacred shrine of hope, as one small part of District Six that none can take away from its people—and as a promise that they will return. Until then, let this plaque be a judgement on those who are destroying this community and an offence to those who let it happen.

- Well, the shrine has stood, together with St. Mark's and the mosques of the District.
- The plaque has witnessed for twenty-one dark years, and no one has been allowed to become comfortable.
- And the promise has been kept. The return has begun.

It was a small blow against a monstrous evil. We know that *apartheid*'s evil did so much more destruction, but the hope was not in vain. This scarred, desolate place is a parable of all of South Africa. Remember the man who, as Minister of Community Development, destroyed this place? As his power grew, P. W. Botha went on to lay waste to so much more. But where is he now? I met him recently where he now lives and asked him if he was happy in the "wilderness." He said yes, and I said I was very glad to hear that![2]

Apartheid will soon be dust and ashes. The time has come for the birth of something new. How will it happen? The final words of that sermon twenty-one years ago, referred to the destroyers of this community:

> *They will one day learn that only the forgiveness of God and the people will save them . . . Father, forgive. . . .*

They haven't quite learned that lesson yet. The state president's actions this week prove that. The Further Indemnity Bill is a disgrace to Mr. De Klerk and to his office.[3] The state president is a lawyer and says he is a Christian. As a lawyer, he doubtless sees the admission of wrong as an invitation to retribution; as a Christian he should know that it is the first step to receiving the grace of forgiveness. Christian theology teaches that forgiveness and reconciliation are possible only if the full truth is known; and, humanly speaking, forgiveness can only be offered by the wounded party.

Mr. De Klerk, you and your colleagues—all those who did the ugly deeds that made *apartheid*—so long as you hide behind your secret amnesty committees, you will never find peace. Come to the people who are here today and say you are sorry. Walk on the weed-grown streets of District Six and mourn for the people you hurt. Read the names of the victims of Sharpeville, Soweto, Sebokeng, Boiphatong, and Bisho. See the seeds of hate and violence you sowed on the hills of Natal and among the shacks of Crossroads and Phola Park—and say, "We are guilty."[4]

And let the people you hurt—let them pronounce forgiveness. *No one else can.*

And what of the future? It is not only the forgiveness of the past that must come from those who bore the pain; I believe that the best hope for the future is also in their hands.

If you visit the Vietnam Memorial in Washington, D.C., the only war memorial I know that doesn't glorify war—you enter it by walking down a sloping path with a low wall of black marble alongside you. You descend deeper as you walk, and the wall gets higher until it towers above you. And you see that it is covered in names, fifty thousand of them. Each is a young man or woman who died in that terrible, wasteful war. And as you stand there, the horror of it overwhelms you, and you feel deeply the sins and suffering of humanity. Then the path begins to rise again and the wall gradually reduces in size, until you come out onto ground level—and you are different. You have descended into the pain and death of humanity's cruelty and folly, but you are still alive and your life is still yours, to live differently.

As we begin to put into place the building blocks of a new District Six and a new South Africa, let the names of those who have suffered be before us and let the survivors of the struggle ensure that we will be different. Today we have descended into one of the memories of what the great wall of *apartheid* did. Let us come back to the surface now, determined that the future will be different.

A favorite piece of sacred music that never seems to lose its appeal is "The Holy City." We used to sing it in this beautiful old church. One of its verses tells us about the kind of city that God wants to see rise on the ruins around us where so many were cast out:

> The light of God was on its streets,
> The gates were open wide;
> And all who would might enter,
> And no one was denied.
> No need of moon or stars by night,
> Nor sun to shine by day;
> It was the New Jerusalem,
> That would not pass away![5]

That is the future we must commit ourselves to now, a future where the gates will never shut anyone out again, where they will be flung wide open and all will enjoy the right to walk these streets in the light of God.

---

1. The Group Areas Act forced different race groups into separate residential areas and was the instrument used to remove all people of color from District Six.

2. Botha retired to a coastal town called "Wilderness"—hence the pun.

3. De Klerk, in spite of his courageous turning away from *apartheid* in 1990, played a dubious and wily game between then and the first democratic elections in 1994. The Further Indemnity Bill was an attempt to wipe out accountability for past government crimes without revealing what they were. It was very different from the Truth and Reconciliation process that finally emerged.

4. These places each represented a dimension of black suffering during the *apartheid* era.

5. F. E. Weatherly, "The Holy City."

In the Crucible with God and a Good Preacher

Having urged Peter Storey to share some of his sermons with the rest of us, I was delighted to receive this collection on a September day in 2001. Here, in these powerful sermons, is a portrait of a faithful preacher and his people with God in the crucible.

I had urged Peter to give short introductions to his sermons, setting them in historical context for contemporary readers, that is, readers post *apartheid*. Yet in reading these sermons in September 2001, I soon realized that I had underestimated Peter's power as a prophet. What we read here is more than an historical record of one good preacher in a tough time past. Here is a word for today.

I read these sermons in the immediate aftermath of our terrible Tuesday when the earth shook and great towers fell in New York. The homiletical response to the horror was not immediately encouraging. Falwell and Robertson took turns blaming this on abortionists, gays, and others who had dismantled "Christian America." Flags were unfurled in churches all over America on the next Sunday; we all stood and sang the national anthem, Billy Graham reassured the nation's powerful gathered at the National Cathedral that we were all innocent, and the president mounted the pulpit to call for all-out war to eradicate evil. For my part, I preached a mostly therapeutic meditation with vague reference to grace, mercy, healing, and other liberal virtues.

Then Peter preached. Reading his sermons from the crucible of South Africa, I did not know whether to be encouraged or ashamed about my sermons.

Bishop Tutu has rightly praised Peter's eloquence and courage. Here, in epilogue, I would like to say a word for his theology. Peter's wise father told him that "everything begins in theology and ends in politics." True. Yet I find it remarkable that, almost without fail, Peter always begins his sermons with God, with a strong biblical directive. This uppity preacher who refuses to be servile to the powers-that-be is courageously subservient to Scripture. While nearly all of these sermons are courageously, pointedly "political," they are, first of all, biblical. He defers to God early and often in his sermons, which enables him to say something fresh and interesting, as fresh today as when he first preached it in the crucible. His father taught him that racism is not simply a racial, economic, social problem but also a "sin against God"; and Peter never let his congregation forget it. His theological subservience gives him the fine freedom to give a scathing rebuke to both Mr. De Klerk and to Ms. Mandela. He nails them, not just for their political mistakes but for their sin. So in love is he with the Church's peculiar speech that he is unashamed to use it even when testifying to a government commission. We who have been urged recently to jettison our Christian language for more allegedly "public theology" take note. Our language does quite well when linked to a life (this courageous pastor and bishop) whose expansive, suffering witness gives substance to our speech.

To those who attempt to make the conventional distinction between the loving, caring "pastor" and the truthful, disruptive "prophet," Peter presents a critique of this unbiblical disjunction. He is a pastor to the core, not some roving, raving itinerant. His prophecy is a function of his pastoral care. Some of his most unflinching diatribes are directed at his own congregation. When his people complain that he has been "too dramatic" in his opening sermon, Peter fires back the next week with a confession that perhaps he was "not strong enough" in last Sunday's sermon in the bloody aftermath of the June 16 massacre in Soweto.

"They Have Damned Their Souls" is a marvelous piece of pastoral rhetoric. Pastor Storey offers no false or cheap consolation. He names names. He is righteously indignant, angry with the perpetrators, consoling to the victims, and extravagant in referring all to the ultimate triumph of the righteousness of God.

Conventional pastoral wisdom tells us to keep a lid on things during congregational crisis. Rather than throw water on glowing coals, to soothe, reassure, or moderate, Peter turns up the heat, fans the flames of the crisis, names names, rants, rebukes, tugs on the emotions, resorts to poetry; thus he turns the congregational fear and uncertainty into a joyous sense of being privileged to be part of God's great pageant of redemption.

I was not at all surprised that Peter's favorite prophet appears to be Jeremiah. Like Jeremiah, he can blast. He can comfort. And never does he resort to the easy healing of deep wounds (Jeremiah 8). Even on the road, he will thank Methodists at Lake Junaluska for their support and then rebuke them with a Jeremiad for having a flag in their sanctuary—but in such a way that you know that they will invite him back to preach next summer.

The pastor in Peter seems to lead him, in almost every Sunday sermon, to end his sermon with specific, definite things that ordinary Christians can do in order to be part of the redemptive work of Jesus. Thus, his prophecy is never simply abstract exhortation, but always a pastoral attempt to ask, in an apocalyptic age, in the crucible, "How then shall we live?"

I shall never forget the joy, the deep, pervasive joy, experienced throughout the congregation, when Peter preached "When God Turns the Tide" in Duke Chapel in 1990. One does not get that sort of ecstatic, triumphant joy that often in our Church. At least, not when I preach.

So, here in September, in the American church's turn to walk through the fiery furnace and our time to hear sermons in a time of struggle, I give thanks for the words and witness of Peter Storey. It takes a deep theological acumen to know that one is with God in the crucible, it takes great grace to know God's word amid the struggle, and even greater grace for the guts to speak it.

The Reverend Dr. William H. Willimon
Dean of Duke University Chapel